BDSM for Writers

By

Dr. Charley Ferrer

Published by
The Institute of Pleasure
PO Box 60985
Staten Island, NY 10306

ISBN: 09770063-9-5
International ISBN: 978-09770063-9-7

eBook ISBN: 0-9770063-8-7
International eBook ISBN: 978-0-977063-8-0

Library of Congress Catalog Card Number: Pending

Manufactured in the United States

Cover Designer: Heidi Hutchinson

Cover Art: Fotolia, Capture Erotica, Starblood

Editor: Casey Lynn

www.bdsmforwriters.com

For all the authors, published and unpublished,
who open the door to our hearts
and mind and remind us
what it's like to fall in love

Table of Contents

Preface

I've written BDSM romance for over a decade. During that time, I've had the privilege of seeing it evolve into a popular, diverse category of erotic romance, a genre that has arguably contributed to the sexual empowerment of its mostly female readership. In those ten years I have learned one thing for certain. To write BDSM romance well, an author *must* have a true sense of the underlying psychology. Knowing the difference between this or that sex toy is important, but to really pull the reader into the story, an author must sympathetically comprehend Domination/ submission (D/s) so that she can help her readers connect to the emotions and motives of her characters practicing it. One of the maxims of BDSM romance is that a quality D/s story doesn't require the presence of a single whip, chain or rope because psychology is 90% of Domination/submission interactions (though having those elements can certainly make it more fun!).

To my knowledge, this is the first book specifically targeted toward writers of BDSM romance. Dr. Charley integrates both the psychology and the mechanics, introducing examples that help explain their symbiotic relationship. She doesn't just tell you what a flogger is; she lets you know why a Dominant would pick it up, or a submissive desire to feel its strike on his or her flesh. She presents these explanations in a personal, informal discussion format, versus imparting a set of detached facts. Through this approach, she liberally scatters seeds of opportunity for story/character development. The information in *BDSM for Writers* makes BDSM relevant to the world of BDSM romance, giving extreme and less extreme examples of BDSM practice so an author can move along the spectrum, depending on what sparks his/her muse.

Beyond the taboos normally associated with BDSM, there is of course an enduring prejudice that a Dominant woman is a psychotic man-hater with issues to resolve, or a submissive woman is a traitor to her own gender, wanting to take us back to the days when women only had the rights that men gave them. Dr. Charley explains why those theories are misguided, as well as defines the different levels of participation in Dominance and submission—from the dabblers spicing up a relationship, to the person truly D/s oriented. With her different, more empathetic glimpse into this world, Dr. Charley demonstrates why the heroes and heroines of BDSM romance novels are gaining such a strong readership among women.

This very validating book is an excellent addition to the writers' toolbox. It is a resource I feel will contribute to the continuing growth of quality BDSM romance fiction. As a reader as well as writer of that genre, I wholeheartedly support that effort!

Joey W. Hill

A note from the Author

As I started to write this book, I found myself constantly rewriting the first chapter and editing my comments as I struggled to discover the correct approach to impart the valuable information every author who writes about Dominance and submission and the BDSM lifestyle should know. I wanted to ensure that I not only covered the basic fundamental aspect of BDSM (Bondage, Discipline, Sadomasochism) but also helped the reader—who would become the writer—understand the vast complexities of this unique subculture and lifestyle that is all too often misunderstood, pathologized, and discriminated against.

Okay, I'll admit it, I also found myself pretty intimidated writing a book

for WRITERS, and when you add in the fact that many of these authors are *romance writers*, well honestly…I was hyperventilating. I feared my words would be dry and lifeless, not at all as clever and enticing as all my favorite authors. Talk about writer's block!

After a month, the therapist in me realized I was avoiding writing this book and made me face the pink elephant in the corner. As most writers know, there comes a point when we have to kick ourselves in the butt and snap out of it. It also helped that a close friend reminded me I wasn't writing a "romance", I was writing a no-nonsense sexuality book providing the reader with an unbiased look into the world of Dominance and submission. Now non-fiction sexuality I can write!

Okay, now I could breathe again.

So, I tossed out everything I had written and began anew.

Before I open the doors and pull back the wizard's curtain to reveal the amazing diversity in the world of BDSM—Dominance and submission—through this book, I first want to remove the veil of myths and misconceptions which obscure your view.

Through *BDSM for Writers* you will discover the tremendous love and respect shared by individuals who embrace this lifestyle. You will better understand the emotional and psychological connections which are the foundation of a BDSM relationship and begin to comprehend the amazing dynamics associated with men and women in this lifestyle. I hope that, as you learn a few of the intricacies inherent in several of the primary personality types, it'll enable you to breathe that same emotional connection, fire, and intensity into your characters.

As you look further behind the wizard's curtain, you'll begin to understand how these unique relationships can burn so brightly, so quickly, and so intensely. More importantly, you'll discover for yourself that BDSM is neither merely a sexual alternative or sexual fetish which men and women outgrow with time, nor some type of pathological illness they're suffering from, but a healthy and positive way of life to be embraced and cherished—just like any other.

In order to accomplish my goals and provide you with a true representation of the BDSM community, as well as dispel the plethora of myths and misconceptions to enable you to peek behind the wizard's curtain, or in this case behind the Leather one, I cannot write this book from an impartial technical *how-to* perspective. As with all my other books on sexuality, I must speak honestly and with authority. And though I can do that in this book from a Sexological perspective based on my extensive knowledge of sexuality, psychology and mental health, I can't provide you with the full flavor of the lifestyle without *outing myself* and allowing you to share a few personal experiences which I have observed or participated in over the years, which will help make this amazingly intimate, and for some—emotionally sacred path—more understandable for you.

So, regardless of *what side of the Whip* you're on, whether you're new to the BDSM lifestyle, a full-fledged participant, or have dabbled slightly now and then (merely obtaining research *chuckles*), you will find the information in *BDSM for Writers* valuable and enlightening as it opens a door into a world most misunderstand, fear, and discriminate against, perhaps because of their own hidden and/or denied desires.

I have no doubt *BDSM for Writers* will become one of your definitive resource guidebooks to creating the heart of these types of characters in your novels (not only in romance but in every other genre) as you return to it repeatedly to review the intricacies of Dominant and submissive personalities. Feel free to use any of the examples provided as you create your own characters. Use the *BDSM Checklist for Writers* I've created as a guide to creating your characters' personality traits, their desires and fears, and even as a resource to help you build scenes and erotic interactions. The *BDSM Checklist for Writers* will also provide you with food for thought on the various implements used to erotically heighten sensations and the various possibilities of combining positions with erotic toys to create different emotional and physical experiences. Purchase a copy as a gift for a friend and/or fellow writer to help them along with their research and discovery.

Before we get into the heart of the book, I want to address two very important issues—disclaimers if you will.

First, I am not a romance writer. My background is on sexual behavior, education and self-empowerment. I hold a Masters in Counseling Psychology, a Doctorate in Human Sexuality, and certification as a Clinical Sexologist and Erotologist. I am at the top of my field and have the distinguished honor of being the only Latina Doctor of Human Sexuality in the United States *at the moment*. My first book, *The W.I.S.E. Journal for the Sensual Woman*, won the award for Best Self-Help Book in 2002. *BDSM for Writers* will be my eighth non-fiction book on sexuality. Basically what all those credentials mean is that I know more about sex then I ever wanted to know. Well ok, maybe I haven't yet learned all I wanted to know since I'm still conducting research on ancient sexual tribal customs as well as modern sexual behavior studies through the *Institute of Pleasure*, so maybe in another twenty years I'll be closer to knowing it all.

My point is, I know the intricacies of sex and can solve most any problem associated with it. However, I know nothing about writing romance. Thus, this book is not about the technical aspects of writing a romance. I will not attempt to discuss character and/or plot development nor how to keep the romance and suspense going in your novel. Just thinking about the complexities of such a feat makes me hyperventilate. I will not discuss ways to write your novel to keep the reader engaged. Nor will I address grammar and sentence structure. For someone as dyslexic as I am, that's just a nightmare to even contemplate. I will leave it up to you to create those fabulous stories which keep me on the edge of my seat and keep me titillated with all those lovely flowery adjectives romance writers use to describe passion and sex. Though I really do love when you're not so politically correct or proper and just *talk dirty* to me!

If you're just starting out as a writer, I'll refer you to those wonderful organizations which exist, such as Romance Writers of America (RWA), that help women and men embrace their dreams of becoming published authors and provide all the how-to's necessary to create a great novel, as well as all the local writers' workshops in your area.

What I will share with you in *BDSM for Writers* are the sexual aspects and psychological make-up of individuals who participate in Dominance and submission to help you become a creditable writer of BDSM romances. Throughout the pages of this book, I will provide you with examples of various behaviors and share with you actual experiences which I've observed or engaged in, and others I've considered from discussions with fellow lifestylers so that you may get a true feel and accurate flavor of what BDSM is truly all about. No, I will not reveal to you which is which. *(*winks and smiles*)*

I will, however, encourage you to go out and discover BDSM for yourself. Encourage you to do your own research. To interview men and women who actively participate in the lifestyle. I encourage you to attend demonstrations, even take a few workshops on how to throw a *Whip* or how to *Flog* someone. You'll discover for yourself how truly difficult it is to throw a Whip while in four-inch heels—

wearing flats or doing it barefoot is so much easier and primal. Volunteer to be a *practice dummy,* as we like to call those who let the Dominants experiment and learn various techniques on them. Discover for yourself what it's really like to stand in a room among individuals who embrace their sexuality in all its glory and are not ashamed, those who are brave enough to share it with others as you voyeuristically observe them in action.

Give yourself permission to explore!

I will also share with you a *BDSM Checklist for Writers* which I've created specifically for you, which will help you create a few scenarios of your own and give you food for thought when considering what deliciously wicked toys to use and in what manner, or what compromising situation you want to thrust your characters into. I will provide you with a list of reference books and materials which I've read myself and feel comfortable recommending to anyone entering this unique lifestyle. I've even provided you with a few organizations and facilitators I feel confident can assist with your exploration. And, of course, I'll refer you to my workshops and the upcoming *BDSM for Writers* Conference specifically designed to provide you with hands-on

experiences as well as discussions with lifestyle practitioners and play time with some BDSM equipment. Most of all go out and discover things for yourself! It's the only way to really learn.

Secondly, this book is not intended to be a *beginner's guide to BDSM*, though it provides an excellent introduction into the lifestyle. Use it instead as a guide to understanding this unique psychological mindset and culture.

For legal purposes, I'm always required to inform you that engaging in BDSM activities is both emotionally and physically risky and that some levels/extremes are dangerous and can result in serious injury and/or death. As with anything else that involves some risk, you should not only make the choice a conscious one that works for you, but ensure to educate yourself by researching and joining the various BDSM organizations available throughout the United States and abroad.

Use the information in *BDSM for Writers* as a starting point for discovery. I give you permission to research to your heart's content any aspect of sexuality that you wish and encourage you to return to share it with me and others so that we may all grow in our knowledge. Use the most powerful phrase in any language and let it open up a world of possibilities. Repeat it after me: **"I am doing research!"**

I hope the information provided in *BDSM for Writers* helps you create a romance novel that BDSM practitioners and lifestylers will enjoy reading. Yet more importantly, I hope that those individuals who are just learning about BDSM or discovering it personally for the first time through your novels—especially those men and women who identify as having these unique erotic desires—can see themselves portrayed in a positive, healthy manner and not be filled with shame or feel they are portrayed as the sick and perverted monsters of ages past.

Now let's take an unbiased look at the world of *Dominance and submission* and strip away the Hollywood veneer of the Dominatrix cracking her *Whip* at sniveling males who want nothing more than to lick her boots; pathetically submissive females who let men walk all over them; and the plethora of misconceptions perpetuated by novelists who had no knowledge of the complexities of this extremely erotic lifestyle so we can enjoy the adventurous allure behind the Leather, the Whip, and the essence of love, sex, and romance that is the BDSM lifestyle.

Dr. Charley Ferrer

Chapter 1

BDSM in Our Daily Lives

It might amaze you to realize that BDSM is not all that uncommon among the general population. I dare say everyone has participated in some form of basic BDSM practices repeatedly throughout their lifetime, either during childhood, in their teens, or within various relationships and family structures. The only difference is that the general population hasn't given their behavior a name.

It's imperative to remember that not everything derived from these activities was sexual in nature. Sometimes participating in them brought a sense of balance and comfort in an otherwise chaotic world. At times the individual doesn't even realize why his or her need is almost a compulsion or why it feels "normal" to do so.

What are these sadomasochistic practices?

Below are a few of the most common examples, both sexual/sensual and non-sexual in nature, which are steeped in BDSM dynamics.

Have you ever given your lover a hickey or received one from them? Why? Wasn't it to ensure everyone knew that he *belonged to you*?

And what about those times that your partner told you, "If you do that again, you'll get a spanking." Did you behave or did you purposely—blatantly—do it again hoping he would carry out his threat, teasing him just a little bit more, calling his bluff? Or was it so you could receive those love taps which for "some reason" excited you?

What about those times when you begged him to thrust harder as he held you against the wall, driving you wild? Or was it you who pinned him to the bed or couch, riding him wildly until you reached your release, instructing him on how you wanted him to move and touch you?

Did you ever wrestle with your partners or with other kids when you were younger because you enjoyed the sense of power and control it gave you, if only for a few moments as you pinned him? Did you enjoy it when the boys blushed because they couldn't control their bodies' reactions? Just who pinned who—and how?

Do you recall that boy who let you put make-up on him to become your living "doll"? Or the one who let you tie him up when you played Cowboys and Indians or Cops and Robbers?

These are all forms of Dominance and submission as well as sadomasochism. Let me break them down for you.

Those hickies you gave to your partner which you bragged about, proudly showing everyone that you "marked your territory", were signs of *ownership*. Signs to let others know your partner was taken and not to touch him. And those hickies you received which you proudly flaunted revealing the "treasure" kept hidden under your turtleneck sweater or a scarf so your parents wouldn't ground you, were a sign of acceptance, of affection. A sign which you promptly rubbed in the faces of those girls you didn't like or who had an interest in what "you claimed" for yourself. It was a sign you belonged to another. The only difference between a hickey and a collar is the conscious adult acceptance of that claiming: acknowledging you belong to another or he belongs to you. And in lieu of a hickey, in the BDSM community you wear a collar around your neck.

Those feelings of excitement at his threat of a spanking which made you tighten your *tush* in anticipation, and purposely repeat the behavior, was a desire to engage in the *power exchange* with another individual. To push against their control and have them correct you or show you their dominance. If you were providing the *Spanking*, slapping his *tush*, was it the shock on his face that sent those tingles through you, or was it the way he pushed you to give him more?

What about those times that you wrestled the boys (girls) to the ground? What did it do for you? Was it the power you held over them, pinning them to the floor, knowing that you could pit your strength against theirs and win—or even better, have them surrender? And when they became stronger, was it still exciting to have them wrestle with you, to feel the excitement in their body, to know you were the cause of it? Know that you could control all that strength with a look or a touch, eliciting their surrender…their submission? Or did you enjoy being pinned to the ground beneath him? These were the beginnings of the *Power Exchange*. Not necessarily sexual in nature when you were younger, but instead a way to test your dominance or the dominance of another.

What about those rare boys that allowed you to paint their faces, put eye shadow and lipstick on them? Those that took comfort in letting you lead and following your wishes and at times your demands? That young submissive boy who swore you to secrecy or struggled beneath you as you wrestled on the ground while you threatened to put lipstick on him and he didn't find the strength to merely push you off him despite being able to? No, he wasn't necessarily gay or a transvestite, but perhaps an awakening submissive wanting to do things to please a friend—a young Dominant.

Then there were the boys and girls who loved to be tied up. Whether to prove they were strong or merely because it felt good to be that vulnerable and trust that the other person would keep them safe. Then again, there were boys and girls who just loved to tie up someone else. Little Dominants and submissives in action!

We all start out somewhere. These behaviors were there in childhood even if they weren't widely acknowledged, shared, or understood.

And when you beg your partner to thrust into you harder, needing his strength, needing to feel owned, to tap into that primal wildness, this is just another level, another plane, of your desires to engage in an exchange of power that feeds those desires and makes you want more. A *power exchange* that brings you closer to each other.

It is this same unconscious need for the *Power Exchange* that leads couples to fight, to engage in those senseless arguments which lead to incredible *make-up sex*. Because during *make-up sex* there's the unwritten rule that you can be as wild, uninhibited, and *aggressive* as you desire and your partner will not *hold it against you*. Ironically, it is this same aggressive, uninhibited behavior that is common and encouraged and is the underlying dynamics of the BDSM community.

As I hope you are beginning to realize, the *vanilla* and the BDSM worlds aren't very far apart from each other. They merely have a veneer of semantics in naming behavior and a willingness to step outside the norm.

Norm should never to be confused with normal!

Always keep in mind that "norm" refers to a commonly accepted form of interaction or behavior and "normal" is regulated and connected to pathology and, subconsciously, to judgment.

Just because BDSM practices are not the norm in our society doesn't necessarily dictate that its practitioners are abnormal or perverted. I remember when it wasn't the norm for women to wear pants in the 1960s and early 1970s. Yet that didn't mean the women who did were perverted or pathological. Now, no one even blinks when a woman wears shorts.

I'm sure you have your own examples and perhaps your own curiosities about this unique lifestyle. As you read *BDSM for Writers*, allow yourself to view the information and examples provided with an open heart and mind. Remember, just because you may not agree with the practice or certain aspects of it doesn't mean it's wrong.

I wouldn't presume to tell you that everyone in the BDSM community practices or participates in these activities from a place of love, caring and respect; the truth is, there are those in this community (as in any other community) that do so from an angry and even pathological perspective. My hope is that as you create your characters and write your romances you'll show the lifestyle with the dignity and respect it deserves.

Chapter 2

BDSM Fundamentals

BDSM is the acronym most commonly used to identify this community. It stands for Bondage, Discipline, Sadomasochism. BDSM incorporates various mental and physical aspects of interactions between individuals, both male and female, on various different levels, including but not limited to emotional, psychological, physical, spiritual, and sexual. Though this acronym and definition is the most common identifier of the BDSM community and encompasses all aspects, there are other identifiers as well, with different emotional and psychological connections. Among these are Dominance and submission and being Master and slave.

It's important to realize that even within the community itself there is a hierarchy of interactions and different acceptance levels, as well as commitment to interactions and a belief system, between these three very distinct yet similar entities. For the purpose of simplicity, I will use BDSM and Dominance and submission (D/s) interchangeably throughout this book. Master/slave interactions and aspects will be addressed separately due to their unique nature and specific rules when appropriate.

BDSM is used to encompass the entire community and includes Dominance and submission as well as Master/slave aspects, on an emotional or commitment level. BDSM itself is thought of as a place where some individuals who enter the community and want to merely *play* at Dominance and submission remain, never really moving into the more emotional and spiritual connections of this lifestyle--such as relationships which incorporate Dominance and submission or the Master/slave mentality.

BDSM also includes those individuals, both men and women, who merely come into the lifestyle wanting to dabble into their fetish for a little while, or just want some kink in their sex lives but aren't interested in embracing the deeper emotional connections. Thus, these individuals are in the community to literally Roleplay at a fantasy before they turn their backs once more and return to the *vanilla* community. These individuals are not thought of highly within the community as they are seen as "kids in a candy store grabbing as many treats as they can before running back to their vanilla life." The majority of individuals merely dabbling in the lifestyle remain at this entry level of emotional and physical interactions. (*Vanilla* is what lifestylers call individuals who are not into the BDSM lifestyle.)

As for individuals who identify and embrace BDSM's unique psychological and emotional needs and desires, they'll become more discerning in their *play* and interactions and eventually enter into a "romantic/emotionally based" relationship—moving into a Dominance and submission relationship/lifestyle.

Still other practitioners of BDSM will move into a more emotionally and spiritually binding connection which requires more psychological interactions and a greater level of surrender and control, entering into the higher levels of Dominant/submissive and Master/slave relationship.

It's imperative to understand that BDSM is a distinct community with its own belief system and even its own psychological make-up. In a nutshell, it is not only an alternative lifestyle but an actual way of life. Unfortunately, as with any other sexual alternative lifestyle, it is mired in superstition and misconceptions as well as fear and contempt from those *outside* of it and, sadly, some within as well. Individuals participating in BDSM or accepting it as a way of life are often declared incompetent or seen as degenerates. Much like the decades before when lesbians and gays were discriminated against because of their sexual identity, BDSM practitioners are discriminated against in the same manner, many losing their children, their jobs, even their family's support when they are discovered.

There is still a belief that sadomasochistic desires are based on psychological and pathological problems, and in some cases this is true. However, the majority of individuals who practice BDSM are not suffering from psychological problems nor are they axe murders-in-training. They are merely men and women, such as yourself, who have a different *Love Map* connection and express their sexual desires in different, more passionate, primal, and creative ways. They are men and women who explore and even embrace all aspects of their sexual desires including those darker needs which Sigmund Freud called *Thanatos* and which do not conform to nor are accepted by the social norm.

Yes, there are individuals who commit acts of violence that incorporate sadistic practices like torture, humiliation, degradation, objectification—practices often embraced within the BDSM community. However, the major distinction between pathological behavior and normal eroticism is intent and consensuality.

As we discuss the psychology of BDSM, I hope you keep an open mind. Not everyone who engages in Dominant or submissive activities has a pathology. And though there is a misconception that individuals identifying as submissive or slaves have the need to be "abused" or to surrender their will to another because of past childhood traumas or an underdeveloped identity issue, this is not true. The truth is that these individuals wish to experience their lives in deep connection with another. To serve the needs of those they love and respect. To make their loved ones' lives happy and fulfilled. (Sounds like the same reasons people get married, doesn't it?)

I will allow you to research the psychological make-up and the numerous psychological theories on this topic on your own, as that is not the focus of this book. I will, however, address the essential truth needed for you to write your romance—what BDSM is NOT!

BDSM is not Domestic Violence!

In BDSM, when an individual calls out their *Safeword* and says they've had enough, all interactions come to a halt. In domestic violence, there is no respect shown and the individual's request for the abuse to end is ignored. In

BDSM there is never a desire to injure your partner nor be malicious! In domestic violence there is no regard for the partner being assaulted. These two vastly distinct behaviors should *never* be confused.

In BDSM there are safeguards established and honored by its participants to minimize injuries in some of the riskier activities. In fact, the majority of BDSM practitioners educate themselves on First-Aid techniques. They also ensure to learn the proper use of the equipment they will use to stimulate erotic sensations in their partner to minimize and avoid injuries. An abuser, on the other hand, doesn't care what the end result of his violent outburst is.

BDSM is, at its core, all about *Power Exchange*. It is the physical and emotional manifestation of these interactions which leads to a mental or physical release as well as the deep emotional bond possible with another human being. This power dynamic is what creates affection, acceptance, and connection. It is through this exchange that the relationship flourishes and is solidified. Each member in the relationship is responsible for maintaining their role and interacting appropriately. Much the same as the traditional roles of husband and wife, the Dominance and submission (D/s) relationship is based on the foundation of these two roles to ensure its success.

There are very few rules in BDSM. This is a lifestyle where individuals make up the rules as they go and live within an honor system of their own making. This is no different from any other society. However, there are two fundamental rules that all respectful and honorable practitioners observe. These two rules are based on the observation of the *Safeword* and the principle of SSC/RACK.

Rule #1: *Safeword*

A *Safeword* is always observed—under SSC—especially when interacting with a new play partner. This is a designated word, previously agreed upon by the individuals interacting, which will call a halt to all activities. Once the *Safeword* is called, the Dominant will communicate with the submissive about the submissive's needs, fears, and desire to either end the interaction, modify it in some way, or attend to a specific need before continuing. Honoring the *Safeword* shows respect. Those that don't, tend to be ostracized or seen as a danger within the community. When in a public setting, others will come to the aid of the individual who calls out their *Safeword* if the Dominant does not stop.

However, for individuals in established relationships, a *Safeword* may be "pushed", delayed, or disallowed in some instances when involved in a RACK relationship or if the relationships falls under consensual non-consensuality rules. *Safewords* are not permitted for individual who are considered "property" as "property" has only those *rights* designated by their Owner. In these instances, the Master/Mistress/Owner will determine when enough is enough. No, the line into abuse is not crossed as the Dominant is not out to injury the individual but merely "push" the slave slightly further. (You'll understand this concept a little further as we continue.)

Rule #2: SSC/RACK

Your level of commitment and comfort with the individual, your relationship status, trust, prior interactions with the other person, sadomasochistic desires, emotional maturity, and your internal acceptance, will all govern your level of interactions and whether you will agree to SSC or RACK.

SSC stands for Sane, Safe, and Consensual. This is the basic standard by which the majority of individuals in the lifestyle interact and is one of the fundamental aspects of BDSM. It is what is taught to *newbies* entering the scene and is reinforced, for legal and ethical reasons, in all books on BDSM.

Another fundamental aspect of BDSM is RACK, which stands for Risk Aware Consensual Kink. It is understood that participating in any aspect of BDSM has emotional and physical risks involved, and that one must be consciously aware of these risks and consensually choosing to engage in them. Individuals who participate in RACK activities often engage in more advanced levels and aspects of mental and physical *play* which push the boundaries of SSC and are viewed by the community as *Edge Play*. RACK also has an underlying fundamental aspect of *consensual non-consensuality* to varying degrees, which in itself is highly debated within the community and falls into extreme levels of physical and emotional interactions.

The basic concept of *consensual non-consensuality,* an advanced form of BDSM *Edge Play*, is the fact that you willingly and consciously consent NOT to have any rights to object to what is done to you. Thus, you consent beforehand to potentially non-consensual interactions governed by another individual and whatever he or she deems desirous and/or appropriate. This is not something recommended or typically engaged in by *newbies*. Even some experienced practitioners do not enter into this realm. Consensual non-consensuality is like the difference between a Dominant and a Sadist. They're both dominant however one is much more extreme. Individuals who participate in this level of interaction typically play at higher levels of intensity; both emotionally and physically. It is important to remember, this level of interaction is an individual choice.

Most lifestyle practitioners are very ethical and even if a newbie begged ever so sweetly (which is like waving a steak before a tiger), the experienced Dominant engaging with them would not take it to such extreme levels. Thus the true ultimate core foundation of BDSM is Choice! The choice to participate and embrace aspects of yourself that not everyone agrees with or accepts. The choice to experience the various levels of your sexual and emotional vulnerabilities and desires for control and still be accepted, cherished, and even loved.

These emotional and psychological needs are the powerful motivator in all our relationships and what I believe all of us—men and women—whether in the lifestyle or not, long for.

Now that we've discussed the basic fundamentals of BDSM, let's address some definitions so you can better navigate this vastly erotic ocean of personalities and interactions.

Chapter 3

BDSM Definitions

In order to navigate the vast horizons and intricate depths of the BDSM lifestyle you need to have a basic comprehension of its rules, participants, boundaries, and yes, even all those fun erotic toys and props/implements used and incorporated into the deliciously erotic, sensual interactions. Though I cannot cover every aspects of the lifestyle in this book, I will provide you with the major ones. I hope that as you create your BDSM romances these definitions will assist you in building the character aspects you wish to portray and help you present a more realistic heroine as well as all those amazing characters she will interact with.

Please keep in mind that these various roles are interchangeable and can pertain to either a man or a woman, unless they are gender specific, such as in the Daddy or Mommy roles. Some characteristic are interchangeable, as in the case of Switches and masochists, as these individuals incorporate more than one aspect of the following characteristics in their fundamental core make-up. You will notice that I tend to refer to men as the submissive in many of my examples. This is based on my own personal preferences and identification as a Dominant woman. I will try to ensure to vary the roles. However, feel free to change the pronouns around to suit your characters particular tastes. Also, it's imperative to remember that the dynamics of Dominant/Master/Mistress and submissive/slave apply to both heterosexual couples as well as same-sex couples. Finally, not all interactions are based on sexual activities. In fact, some are service-based only and there is no sexual and, at times, no physical contact. It's also not uncommon for a heterosexual Dominant to own a gay/lesbian slave/submissive.

Please bear with me for a few moments as I outline some of the more technical aspects of BDSM and share a few definitions with you. Remember, this is just an outline, a small taste, if you will, of your characters' development and interaction context. You can assign whatever other characteristics you wish them to have. Use the examples provided in *BDSM for Writers* as reference points and build from there.

In order to simplify things as we continue, I will use the terms *BDSM* and *Dominance and submission (D/s)* interchangeably. I will also use *submissive* and *slave* interchangeably unless there is a specific difference between the two levels of interaction. I will do the same with the use of *Master/Mistress* and *Dominant*. It would help to understand that the Master/slave connection is a more structured relationship within the *Power Exchange* and BDSM communities. However, many similarities exist between Dominant/submissive relationships as well and both are just as binding. These relationships would be the vanilla equivalent of marriage.

So, let's get started with a few basic definitions. These are by no means the only terms to know; however, I believe the information below is some of the most important to include. You may notice that my writing style is very personal, so please overlook my jumping from third person to first person. I figure, as the author, you are both the individual learning and the individual observing.

Vanilla:
Vanilla is the term given to anyone who is not in the BDSM lifestyle. Everyone starts out as vanilla. Then your *beans are crushed* as you learn and explore and perhaps even embrace whatever amazing facets of emotional and erotic desires feel comfortable to you.

Power Exchange:
The *Power Exchange* is at the heart of all the interactions shared in BDSM. This is the fundamental core of the relationship, whether from an emotional or physical perspective, which two individuals engage in—one giving,

the other receiving. The *Power Exchange* can be physical, emotional, spiritual, and sexual, or merely service oriented. The actual levels of surrender and control/dominance will vary depending on the individuals and what they desire to share with each other and to what degree.

Newbies:

These are men and women new to the lifestyle. These individuals are often taken under the "community's collective wing" and encouraged to grow and explore, to do their own research, and explore their emotional and psychological connection with various aspects of BDSM. Nowhere else can your emotional connections vary as much as they do within the BDSM lifestyle. It may interest you to know that what you initially see as scary or distasteful and is placed on your list of "never-do's" when you first enter into the community may in time become your most favorite activity or a fetish you cannot do without.

Dungeon:

A Dungeon is where you conduct a *Scene* and/or where you *Play* with your partner. The Dungeon is typically portrayed as a basement or concrete structure, yet in reality it can be anywhere you wish it to be. You can even designate a spare room in your home as your Dungeon room.

Typically, you don't want to have your primary bedroom as your Dungeon unless you live the lifestyle 24/7. Designating a separate room or area as your Dungeon allows for the individuals, whenever they walk into that room, to fall into a psychological mindset which they associate with their experiences in "that area". Unless you live the lifestyle 24/7, you want to cherish down time to decompress and dabble into other aspects of your personality—and your partner's. Plus, the psychological effects of "that room" will serve both the Dominant and the submissive.

Designating a specific room as the Dungeon allows you to have all your toys and accessories available and handy. Nothing stops the flow of a *Scene* faster than having to leave the room to get something you've forgotten.

Some establishments have various themes to their Dungeon or various areas designated for specific *Play*. For example: one area may be designated for medical play and another for Spankings, complete with a Spanking Bench. Some areas will have pulleys or "O" rings on the walls or hanging from the ceiling so you can anchor your slave to these areas and Whip them or tie them up and do other deliciously wicked things to them.

Dungeon Master:

The Dungeon Master's primary function is that of enforcer of club rules. He or She walks about the Dungeon ensuring the rules of the Dungeon are strictly adhered to by all participants. The Dungeon Master doesn't typically interact with others as his/her main role is to monitor all the situations and step in to assist or terminate a *Scene* if he/she feels the Dominant is not experienced enough or has stepped over the limits, or if the submissive demands help or needs it. The Dungeon Master's word is final.

Scene:

This is the name given to the actual interaction between the Dominant and the submissive which is constructed with a specific thought and outcome in mind. A *Scene* may be elaborate and incorporate various protocols and/or rituals as well as assistance or participation from other parties. It can incorporate various erotic objects to elicit sensations, be sexual in nature, or merely be emotional. Then again, a *Scene* may be only based on service and not incorporate any sexual overtures. The *Scene* is whatever the Dominant desires it to be, changing with his/her mood and/or the submissive's response. A *Scene* can last anywhere from a few minutes to a few hours—even a few days.

Play:

The activities shared by two individuals, whether Dominant or submissive, is often called *Play,* regardless of the actual activity. Thus, *Play* can be a Flogging, Whipping, using Candle Wax, etc. *Play* is often not really "play" but merely two individuals sharing and enjoying themselves. It can be carefree and non-restrictive or it can be emotionally and physically intense, depending on the individuals involved. What actually occurs during *Play* is called a *Scene*.

Individuals will often schedule a *Play Date* if they are not living together just as vanilla couples plan dates. *Play Dates* are lots of fun!

Service:

When a submissive or slave is in "service", they are performing a particular activity for the Dominant or their Master/Mistress. Service can be physical or sexual in nature. Service can be anything from a foot massage to cleaning the Dominant's house, or it can be a function the slave/submissive performs, such as running errands. At times, a particular service has accompanying protocols and/or rituals associated with it. This is all determined beforehand by the Dominant.

Collar:

Though collars have become popular accessories worn by teenagers and those into the Goth scene, as well as the vanilla public at large, actual collars are a sacred part of the Dominance and submission (D/s) and Master/slave (M/s) relationships. A collar signifies ownership and acceptance—just as a wedding ring does for married couples.

Nowadays, with everyone going out and purchasing their own collar, it's hard to determine who's a "free" submissive/slave and who's *Owned*. Typically a locked collar means the submissive/slave is *Owned*. You might see a lock on the back of a collar or you'll see a tag handing from the loop in the front of the collar which might state, "Property of…"

The color of a collar also holds significance. The *Old Guard* had many rules concerning color of the collar and levels of service. For example, a light blue collar signifies the person is *in-training* and *under consideration* by someone. Therefore, that person is not available for interactions and if you wish to interact with them, you must go through the Dominant/Master/Mistress that *holds their leash*—the individual the submissive is *under consideration with.* It is not acceptable in the community to touch anyone that is collared or *under consideration/in-training* without obtaining permission first.

Black collars used to signify the individual was free and available but over time it has become the standard color of choice for the community, and both free and owned submissives/slaves use it. Gold and silver collars imply Ownership and a permanent relationship. Although not all permanent Master/slave relationships are denoted by these colors.

Some Masters/Dominants/Mistresses will have a collar specially made. Personally, I created a Native American design for the collar I choose for my partner, with a matching one for myself.

Though typically it is only the submissive who wears the collar, some female Dominants have used collars or "chokers" as fashion accessories. And as I mentioned above, I wear a Native American necklace which has at times been confused with a collar. Therefore, don't let the "collar" fool you. When in doubt, always ask.

Limits:

Limits are the conditions and restrictions placed on acceptable and non-acceptable behaviors or activities which a submissive is willing to conduct/perform during a *Scene.* There are Soft and Hard limits. Both soft and hard limits can be pushed to help the submissive/slave expand his or her ability to endure whatever is being done to them; to push them past a hurdle or emotional release; and/or because it is felt by the Dominant that pushing the limit a bit without crossing over it is acceptable. However, where soft limits are negotiable and may be overcome with time and trust, hard limits should always be honored.

Soft & Hard Limits:

Soft limits are typically placed by the submissive when he or she isn't sure whether or not they would feel comfortable performing/participating in a specific activity. Typically, the activity needs to be tweaked slightly for it to be acceptable. Then, of course, the submissive may merely desire the soft limit to be taken out of his/her control or be forced to engage in the activity so he/she can override the guilt and/or shame associated with it. Soft limits can be broken. You'll often know it's a soft limit because the individual will state, "that's a limit...but if you want to..."

Newbies typically will have a long list of soft limits since they are not sure how they'll feel about a particular activity. (This is where the *BDSM for Writers Checklist* helps; it's a reference point to start from. You may find your character grows in their desires from the beginning of the book to its conclusion; or if you are writing a series, you might find your characters have expanded their horizons and their cravings.)

I often find that individuals merely need some encouragement and assurance that they will not be rejected after performing or participating in activities which may be sexually extreme, outside their comfort zone, outside their designated gender norms, or outside societal norms. (Notice I said *norm* not normal. Everything in BDSM is normal; it just may not be the *norm*.)

And of course, there are loopholes to *soft limits*. An example of a soft limit can be where the submissive states you **cannot** *Spank* him with a hair brush; however there was no "*Limit*" against *Spanking* him with a wooden spoon or a bare hand. Gotta love those loopholes! Or if the slave has a hard limit against Spankings with a belt you can have your Dominant character Spank the slave with a Cane or even a Flogger. Thus, pushing the limit but not breaking it.

Hard limits are an absolute **No!** These are never acceptable to break. Hard limits are something everyone should honor. This goes for both the Dominants and submissives as well.

It should be noted that Dominants can also have limits of their own. These can be based on the same principles as the submissive/slave's limits. In addition, Dominants may impose limits on the behaviors and restrictions the submissive/slave needs to adhere to while in a relationship with them. For instance, the Master/Mistress may impose a requirement (a *hard limit*) that the submissive not interact with any other Dominants while *Owned* by them. Should the submissive break this *hard limit,* he/she would be dismissed or severely punished, or both.

That said, just because you should honor hard limits doesn't mean you can't push them a bit. For instance, if the submissive male has a hard limit about same sex interactions, you can have your character tease him about what it would feel like to watch him with another man. To push the "Mind Fuck" and psychological play further, while performing anal sex with him, the Dominant woman can call her strap-on by a male name.

Dominant:

The Giver. This individual is in charge of the relationship. He or She sets the rules, safeguards their partner, administers training and correction as She/He deems appropriate and desirous in their personal relationship. The Dominant also dictates and administers punishment for any violations of the rules and/or transgressions the submissive may be guilty of. He or She is entrusted with the emotional and physical safety of the individual He/She interacts with. The Dominant is responsible for establishing and reinforcing the protocols of the relationship. Dominants have an alpha personality and are used to being in charge both at work and within the relationship. However, you don't need to be in a management position at work to qualify as a Dominant.

Ironically, most dominant males at work are actually submissive at their cores and more service-oriented women—at work—are dominant at their cores. I think this dichotomy shows the irony of our societal norms.

A female Dominant is often called Mistress unless she chooses another title for herself such as Ma'm, Lady So-and-so, Owner, Master, Goddess, etc. Some Dominants merely use their first names. It is a personal choice. When interacting with his or her Dominant, the slave/submissive will use Ma'm or Sir as honorifics.

There is a small percentage of women who use the title Master instead of Mistress. Personally, I do not like the name Mistress as there is a negative subconscious connation to the word. For some men, there is the expectation that sexual favors are owed to them or that the female Dominant has less value than the male Dominant. There is also the subconscious belief by some men and women entering the BDSM community that a Dominant woman is nothing more than a pseudo-professional Dominatrix and should be considered little more than a prostitute as "She is there to serve the submissive"—in essence giving him a "free" BDSM session.

Most romance novels, if not practically all, designate the woman as Mistress or have her slave call her by her given name such as Mistress Stephanie. It's your story. You choose what you wish to have Her called and by whom.

Proper etiquette dictates that the Dominant is always shown respect, even in written form, by capitalizing their title (Master/Mistress) and their pronouns. For example: using a capital "M" for Master/Mistress anywhere it appears in the sentence and capitalizing any pronouns which relate to the Dominant such as the "Y" in *You* when the submissive is referring to them. A written example is: "The chores *You* requested were performed, Mistress."

The abbreviated version of Dominant is Dom for men and Domme for women.

Master:
These individuals can be either male or female in gender. The level of control and commitment required from their partner is the key in these relationships. Masters tend to be more disciplined and structured than Dominants. There is a higher level of intensity and mastery associated with these relationships. Also, there are standard and individualized protocols and etiquettes which dictate the interactions of a Master and His/Her slave. It is more common for a Master to have several slaves dedicated to various tasks in the Master's home or life than it is for a Dominant to have. Also a Dominant/submissive relationship tends to be more couples only; however there are many Polyamorous households that practice Dominance/submission principles.

There are also separate community and educational functions specifically geared toward the dynamics of Master/slave relationships which are focused on the development of the Master and of the slave, as opposed to

the typical BDSM events and community *Play Parties.*
There is also a belief within the community that as you grow
in maturity and desire for higher levels of interactions with
your submissive, you move from the introduction of BDSM
and mere "play" phase into a Dominant/submissive
relationship, and ultimately to a Master/slave relationships.
Although not all D/s relationships move into the more
restrictive aspects of Master/slave relationships even after
years of cohesive and positive loving interactions; however,
if they do, they still may not consider themselves in a
Master/slave relationship. The beauty of BDSM is its
ambiguous definition, thus leaving it to the specific
individual couple to create the relationship that works best
for them.

Sadist:
Unlike Dominants and Masters, Sadists are not
necessarily interested in the D/s dynamics of the relationship
and may have a more egalitarian interaction and relationship
with their slaves or submissives. Then again, they may be
even stricter in their rules, protocols, and requirements.
Regardless, the Sadist is nonetheless in charge of the
relationship and the Master of it!

The Sadist enjoys pushing the limits and taking the
submissive/slave on a journey of physical, emotional,
psychological, and/or sexual exploration. The Sadist will
often engage in more advanced levels of emotional and
physical interactions such as *Edge Play*. Where a typical
Sadist will push against physical limits and endurances, a*n*
Emotional Sadist will push against the slave's fears and
emotional issues, thriving on *Fear Play* and *Mind Fucks,*
which are the basis of *Psychological Play.*

It should be clearly understood that the Sadist is *not*
attempting to injure the submissive/slave in any way; He or
She is merely interacting at a level others may fear to tread.
Also the Sadist, at times, will push His/Her own limits when
interacting with a slave at various levels and may be
emotionally affected by the same. (Think advance statistical
evasive Ranger training and/or Special Force psychological
training, for a somewhat vanilla comparison).

The Sadist in these interactions is **NOT** interacting in a pathological manner! There is never an intention to **injure** the submissive, merely to share a part of themselves—what they may consider as a sacred part of themselves.

Sadists are typically very discerning and selective in their choice of individuals with whom they will interact, and to what level. Sadists are extremely committed to the safety and well-being of those they interact with. Yes, there are some who aren't; however, there are idiots and dishonorable individuals in all walks of life. As I mentioned before, in these interactions, there is no pathological behavior as there is no malice intended!

I find Sadists to be more loving and attentive to their slaves, especially after an intense *Scene*, ensuring the slave's physical and emotional wellbeing.

The best vanilla analogy I can use to help you distinguish between a Sadist and a Dominant is: A Dominant sometimes needs a "reason" to discipline and punish His or Her submissive/slave—a Sadist merely needs a place. (Smiles, ok maybe that was a bit cavalier, but you get the jest.)

submissive:

The receiver. This individual is the other half of the D/s relationship. He or she follows the rules and is of service to the Dominant. The submissive role is not always sexual in nature. The submissive may be merely providing service to the Dominant in some manner. For example: house cleaner, computer expert services, preparing meals, etc.

It is the submissive's duty to obey and adhere to the dictates of his/her Master/Mistress. The underlying premise is to be of service. As a submissive, he/she typically has more liberties than a slave. One of the major differences between a slave and a submissive is that the submissive is considered a "free" agent and can interact with whomever he or she chooses to until they become the property of another.

Though the submissive may not necessarily be used sexually, they may be used physically. There is a belief by some in the community that submissives are not as dedicated as slaves; however, that is an internal debate within the

33

community and at times becomes a matter of internal dedication and semantics as well as a personal level of surrender.

Another major distinction between a submissive and a slave is that a submissive has rights and the ability to object to certain activities or requirements and can negotiate some aspects within their relationship—setting limits. Thus, in essence, the submissive has more liberties within the relationship than a slave does.

The best vanilla analogy I can provide you with is the difference between a girlfriend and a wife. More is expected from one than the other and some rules can be broken and forgiven of a girlfriend (submissive); however, they would lead to divorce if conducted by the wife (slave), divorce being the equivalent of *dismissal* in a D/s relationship.

In written form it is common practice for a submissive to use a lower case "i" when referring to themselves as they consciously reinforce the decision to see themselves as belonging to another and taking a more submissive/subservient role. Also his/her name is never capitalized. A written example of this is: "Dear Master, i have completed all the tasks You asked of me. Respectfully, joshua."

Please note, this submissive subservient role does not imply less value, but merely a difference in their equality and roles within the relationship. Following the example previously given, a wife doesn't hold less value in a marriage than a husband, merely a different one.

Sub is the abbreviation of submissive.

slave:

These individuals can be either male or female. Their entire purpose is to "be of service" to his/her Master/Mistress and make his/her Dominant's life simpler and happier. The slave gives up many of his/her "rights" (by choice) to allow the Master/Mistress to dictate the slave's interactions and responsibilities within the relationship. Typically, slaves will have set protocols which they are required to maintain in public as well as in private.

Transgressions are met with physical and/or emotional consequences.

The major difference between a slave and a submissive is the ability to deny a Master's dictates. Whereas a submissive may have some say and "veto" privileges within the relationship and/or activity being performed (in the form of *limits*), a slave does not. Also, when interacting in physical and/or sexual activities, the slave has no "rights" to deny what is done or required of him or her. The slave has the *Limits* their Master/Mistress has given them.

Within the relationship, the slave has consciously given his/her agreement to participate in current and future "consensual non-consensual" activities and interactions with his/her Master and others designated by the Master/Mistress in either a physical or sexual nature thus becoming a slave in the true sense of the word.

It should be understood that, though the slave is objectified at times, he/she is very well cared for and held in high esteem and deep affection, even loyalty, from the Master/Mistress. The Master takes his or her responsibility to the slave's physical and emotional well-being very seriously and will guard the slave against any harm.

The slave *belongs* to his or her Master/Mistress!

Typically, though someone may consider themselves a slave, their true connection does not manifest itself until they *belong* and are in a relationship with their Master/Mistress/Dominant. At that point, the slave is no longer allowed to participate nor interact with anyone else without the expressed permission of their Master/Mistress and/or without the Master/Mistress being present during any interactions.

It should be understood that an individual may consider themselves a "slave" but have no Master/Mistress at the moment. The emotional and psychological make-up of a slave is vastly different than that of a submissive. We will address this psychological difference in a later chapter. However, the bottom line is that the fundamental psychological aspect of a slave is to give themselves without reservation because it is in their nature—their very core—to do so, to become enmeshed with their Master/Mistress completely taking their relationship to a deeper more spiritual level.

The proper etiquette for a slave when addressing himself is in the third person. For example: "Master, is it acceptable for *Your* slave to prepare Your bath?" Or it can follow the submissive's format: "After *i* go to the grocery store, *i* will clean Your home."

Masochist:

A masochist is an individual who enjoys the more physical aspects of BDSM. He or she will engage in more physically demanding interactions and *Edge Play* activities. Masochists enjoy riding the waves of pleasure that pain produces in their body. For them, the pain they experience at the hand of their Master/Mistress is an intensely emotional connection as well as a higher level of surrender. Most masochists will not use a *Safeword* as they will allow their Mistress/Master to choose for them when the experience will be over. This level of surrender reinforces their interaction and is often their way of overcoming their fears of the activity or reaching a higher level of consciousness through the acceptance of pain. (This concept of achieving a spiritual connection with the self or another has been in many of our religious beliefs and is a major component of Christianity; remember the common practice of priests reaching divinity through self-flagellation. Or the belief that to "suffer" is a way to reach God.)

A rare subgroup of men and women sometimes fall into the category of *Emotional Masochist.* These individuals thrive on emotional pain and fear. Not all masochists are able to dabble in this realm.

Though most masochists are submissives or slaves, it would be erroneous to classify them all as such. Some masochists have alpha personalities and are very dominant in their own rights, much like the sexual submissives. Thus, these masochists enjoy pitting themselves against their own fears, using the Dominant as their catalyst for this purpose; others merely enjoy the endorphin rush they can experience through pain. There is also the ability, as mentioned before, of working through an emotion—guilt, shame, etc and using pain as the cleanser. In this instance, the masochist is *using* the Dominant as a gateway to overcoming or achieving his goal.

A masochist is considered either a submissive or slave and is treated accordingly. In writing they often use the lower case "i".

Sadomasochist

Some Dominants have masochistic tendencies but not submissive ones. This is what's called a Sadomasochistic personality. This individual enjoys the edgier/darker aspects of physical and/or sexual interactions with his or her slave. Like a switch, they will enjoy giving and receiving pain. However, the major difference between these two personalities is that this Dominant would never surrender their will to their submissive or slave.

For example: the Sadomasochistic Dominant may enjoy giving **and receiving** pain, however he/she would never kneel before their slave nor beg. This Dominant would also never be in servitude to the submissive. These Sadomasochistic individuals may also enjoy allowing their submissive to feel empowered by engaging in rough sex and force; however, at the end of the day, it is the Dominant who will say how much the submissive is allowed to do and when this type of *Play* is over. Plus, a deviously wicked Sadomasochist may even lovingly make *His/Her* submissive pay for his rough treatment of their Master/Mistress at a later date and time thereby reinforcing the power dynamics and their control.

Property/object:

This individual is regarded as lower in status than a slave or submissive and is thought of as the Master/Mistress' *property*. "It" has no rights to object to anything asked of it. It is often objectified and given a *number* (for example: 4663) rather than a name or nickname. Its vanilla name is not used when referring to him/her. It can be used sexually or physically in whatever manner the Dominant decrees. This individual has an internal desire to surrender all and have no opinions, options, or responsibilities aside from those dictated by its Master. This individual is typically found in the most intense levels of BDSM interactions.

The object is referred to in written form as "it" (always in lower case form) and will refer to him/her self in the third person. For example: "Master, *it* will go to the store and *it* will return with all Your required items."

Please note this is not a derogatory position. *Property/objects* are actually highly valued and guarded by their Masters as they are so vulnerable and openly surrender all they are to their Master/Mistress. Such individuals are rare gifts and highly prized by their Owners. However, those who *belong* to disreputable or severely sadistic owners, can be sorely misused in many ways.

Objectification:

Objectification occurs when a submissive/slave is reduced to the sole dictates of his Master/Mistress. In this role, the slave has no rights. They are literally an object for the Dominant's use. He/she (the slave/submissive) is there solely for the purpose assigned, whether that is to serve as sexual stud/whore, to withstand the restraints of a particular role, or to act as particular object (such as furniture or living art—think of the Roman slaves used for this purpose) or for whatever activity the Dominant dictates. Some individuals are objectified in sexual service, others by being designated as furniture, an animal, or something else.

Others forms of objectification can be implemented through the clothing the individual is allowed/required to wear, which strips away his or her identity and provides the slave with another. This may include wearing a full facial hood or taking away his or her name—their identity—and giving them another (typically a number or a "derogatory" name or object name such as *dog* or *whore*). The submissive/slave would then only be referred to as "it" and when referring to "itself" would do so in the third person.

Force is and can at times be used, as well as corporal punishment. Though this interaction may seem derogatory or demeaning, it should be understood that the individual being objectified did voluntarily surrender to begin with and provided his or her consent to the interaction. In essence, they are repeatedly providing their consent to such treatment every time they show up to interact with their Master/Mistress.

This objectification often provides the individual with a sense of well-being and feeling of belonging. Some slaves will objectify themselves in their desire to be of service and to surrender all sense of identity and control to their Master/Mistress. By doing this, they have achieved complete surrender, which is their ultimate goal, what turns them on and/or completes them.

It's essential to keep in mind that what you may judge to be immoral or distasteful, the parties interacting in it find it erotic and freeing. Also, this objectification is not in any way abusive or an example of domestic violence, as the individual was not coerced or forced into accepting this role in the relationship. For the slave/submissive it is what's "right" for them and is an integral part of who they are. As I mentioned previously, BDSM is *not* domestic violence. In a domestic violence situation, the individual would have never chosen to participate in these types of activities; and in BDSM the *property/object* consciously and willingly does so.

Before you pass judgment, it may surprise you to realize that this training and objectification is very similar to how the military trains its new recruits, turning them from civilians into soldiers who obey orders on command— regardless of what that order is.

One of the things to keep uppermost in your mind when engaging in BDSM activities or writing about them is that each individual is different. What feels good and erotic to you may not be perceived in the same manner to another. You are the ultimate judge of what you interact in and as the author of your own BDSM romances, you are the creator of all the relationships.

Switch:
This individual incorporates various aspects of both a dominant and submissive personality. They enjoy both aspects of the *Power Exchange*, though their personality typically falls more onto one side of the Power Exchange

spectrum than the other. Within the community, Switches aren't always seen in a positive light as some believe them to be merely submissives wanting to dabble in domination, or merely someone who wants to casually "play" at the lifestyle. However, others believe that a Switch is able to experience both aspects of the lifestyle, though not as intensely as those who identify as one role or the other. For example, you can sympathize with a woman about what it's like to give birth, however, unless you experience it, you can't completely understand the emotional dynamics associated with it.

It's not uncommon for someone new to the lifestyle to identify as a Switch, as they are unsure where they feel most comfortable.

Many Switches start out/are considered *Service Tops* as they are performing a "service" for another individual and their relationship with or dominance over that individual ends when the *Scene* is over. A Switch would never be considered a Master

Some submissive men new to the BDSM lifestyle will identify as Switches since they feel guilt or shame from being a submissive man. Submissive men often have to combat their own prejudices and those of their counterparts—Dominant men—who may look down upon them for their submission and not consider them "macho" enough. Also, it should be understood that some straight men will accept control and offer service to Dominant men, limiting their interactions to physical interactions and not sexual ones.

Switches can follow either the Dominant or submissive rules for capitalization—they get to choose which protocol to follow. I've often seen them use the lower case "i" when referring to themselves, thus, internally identifying as a submissive.

Sexual submissive:

Though not all submissives or slaves are used sexually, the sexual submissive's primary purpose is sexual interactions with and sexual use by his/her Mistress/Master. However, whereas a submissive will defer the leadership role to their Dominant or be subservient to his/her Master/Mistress in all areas of the relationship, this rule/dynamic is not true of the sexual submissive.

The sexual submissive is typically very dominant in his/her own right and often has an alpha personality in all other areas of his/her life and only relinquish control in sexual matters. Outside amorous interactions, this individual is very opinionated and focused on what they want in life, what they want to share with their partner, as well as the type of "everyday" equalitarian relationship structure they desire to engage in with their "partner".

The sexual submissive may also have very intense masochistic tendencies. However, outside of the sexual arena, their submission is not really present or is minimal. The best example I can provide of this dynamic is the general who goes out and leads his men into battle then gladly surrenders to his lover only to once again take control of his life after that particular interaction is over. He can allow his lover/partner to take the lead in the relationship; however theirs will be more of an egalitarian union than the typical D/s relationship.

Swingers:

These individuals and their lifestyle choice should not be confused with BDSM practitioners. Though some BDSM practitioners share their slaves/submissives sexually with designated individuals, this is not considered swinging. It is at the sole prerogative and discretion of the Master/Mistress to allow or require the submissive/slave's sexual interaction with another person regardless of whether the submissive/slave desired the interaction.

Where the focus for the BDSM practitioners is on *Power Exchange* and the *power dynamics* of that particular sexual interaction, a swinger's primary interest is in sexual interaction—not in establishing a relationship outside their primary one. Swingers do not necessarily engage in BDSM activities, though some do, in addition to swinging. Also, once an interaction with the Dominant/submissive is concluded, there may not be others.

It is rare that you will see BDSM practitioners actively engaging in sadomasochistic practices within a swingers' event as swingers do not typically like to associate with BDSMers. Some Swingers' events even strictly prohibit BDSM activities.

<u>*Safeword:*</u>

It is common practice to give an individual a *Safeword*. This is the word the submissive would call out when they need the *Scene/Play* to pause or come to a complete stop when they have reached their limit. It is the responsibility of the submissive/slave to call out their *Safeword* when necessary. However, Dominants will often "call it" for the submissive or discontinue the *Scene* when the Dominant feels the submissive/slave is unable to continue, or the Dominant wishes to end the interaction with the submissive, for whatever reason.

The *Safeword* is typically a simple word to remember and one that is not normally used in a conversation. For instance, *Carousel...Unicorns...Pumpernickel,* are all good *Safewords*. It can be any word you'd like, although you will want to keep it short and simple and easy to remember.

The *Safeword* cannot be "*No*" or "*Stop*"! These words typically have double meanings and when dabbling in situations where guilt and shame are intermingled with sexual desire, the submissive may feel the need to cry out, "No. Stop!" during a scene, despite their desire to continue. It is more often their sense of guilt and shame, or a programmed response behind the declaration than any true desire to end their interaction. Also, their fear of being rejected or thought of poorly may also generate their need to call a halt to the activities. It is the Dominant's responsibility to ascertain which it is—communication is key.

When interacting with a Dominant for the first time, or if you're not able to remember or come up with a *Safeword*, it's standard practice in the community to use the principles of the *stoplight*—Red, Yellow, Green. This helps guide the Dominant and gives some illusion of control to the submissive. Using Red, Yellow, and Green allows both participants to know the submissive's level of comfort and desire to continue *Playing*.

Let me break it down for you:

- Green means "everything is ok and wonderful, please continue".
- Yellow means the Dominant is pushing boundaries, but the submissive is willing to continue.
- Red calls a halt either to that particular activity or the whole *Scene*.

For example, one slave was happily receiving a Flogging, but when the Dominant began to tickle her she screamed, "Red. Red. I hate tickling." The Dominant immediately ceased tickling, continued Flogging her, and the rest of the *Scene* continued.

SSC:

SSC stands for Safe, Sane, and Consensual. Within the community it is one of the fundamental rules of engagement. Those who break this rule are thought to be "dangerous" and many BDSM'ers will steer clear of these individuals.

Despite the thousands, even millions, of BDSM practitioners in the world, the BDSM community as a whole is still small, and word travels quickly. It is not uncommon for individuals in Texas to know which specific individuals in New York City violated SSC. Also, with the advent of the Internet and the fact that various groups hold events throughout the country and the world, it's easy for word to circulate. The BDSM community has an amazing grapevine.

RACK:

RACK stands for Risk Aware Consensual Kink. Unlike those who practice SSC, individuals who embrace RACK engage in more intense BDSM interactions. These individuals often engage in *consensual non-consensuality* practices and *Edge Play* activities. Individuals who practice RACK may not adhere to the principle that all *Play* stops when a *Safeword* is called by the submissive. This is not because there is no respect or safety measures in place or that the Dominant is being abusive, but is because ignoring or "delaying" the *Safeword* is at the Dominant's sole discretion and prerogative as agreed to under the *consensual non-consensuality* clause negotiated between the Dominant and submissive.

Let's not forget it is the Dominant's prerogative to push the submissive further than he or she thought was possible, whether emotionally or physically. And though it may seem excessive or abusive to you, rest assured that the Dominant is keeping the needs and safety of the submissive uppermost in His/Her mind.

Etiquettes:

Etiquettes are typically the common courtesies used in everyday life, with just a bit more formality. They tend to be individual preferences and can change as needed or desired. Each household has its own etiquettes though standard honorifics are commonplace. When speaking to a Mistress/Master the slave/submissive uses Ma'm or Sir or whatever title the Dominant desires.

Dominant women tend to require typical common chivalrous practices from their slaves, like opening the door for them, seeing to their needs in public, even ordering a meal at a restaurant for them—once the slave has been told what *She,* wants of course.

Protocols/Rituals:

Protocols are a specific way of showing respect. Protocols are specific dictates and behaviors each Dominant or Master establishes for His/Her submissive/slave. This can be anything from how the submissive stands, dresses, or speaks to when these protocols take place. There can be specific protocols for interacting in public as opposed to private settings, as well as rituals for how an individual is required to interact within "vanilla" events in comparison to D/s functions.

For instance, a male slave may be required to go naked with only their collar and cuffs while at home. He may be required to kneel before or stand alongside his Master/Mistress instead of sitting in a chair beside Him/Her. The submissive/slave may be required to obey eye contact restrictions with his Master/Mistress, looking straight ahead or looking down when speaking to Him/Her. This is typical of military protocols, which many individuals in the BDSM community adhere to.

The beauty about a protocol is that you can tailor it to whatever you desire, and if you find that it's not working for you, you can dismiss it and implement another in its place or tweak a specific protocol to work out the kinks in it—no pun intended).

Protocol enforcement is the responsibility of the Dominant and thus keeping them simple is best unless the Dominant is willing to micromanage. It's not surprising that a submissive/slave will sometimes intentionally perform a protocol incorrectly to engage his Master's attention and/or at times to test their Master/Mistress to gauge whether what he (the slave) does is important to their Master/Mistress

Rituals are very rigid, specific, and in some ways sacred. Ritual takes protocol to its ultimate form. Rituals allow slaves to show respect and reverence for the duties they perform for their Master/Mistress and for the interactions they engage in; from typical everyday occurrences such as how they present their Master/Mistress with coffee or present themselves for service (kneeling/standing in a specific manner) to how they prepare themselves physically for *Play* and/or sexual interactions.

Dismissal:
Dismissal is the term used for a BDSM "break-up" that ends the relationship, regardless of the reason behind it. When a slave/submissive is dismissed, his/her collar is removed.

Typically a Dominant will not reinstate a submissive who was dismissed from service in the past especially if their dismissal was based on hard limits imposed by the Dominant being broken. For example, if the submissive was not allowed to interact in physical or sexual play with another individual, but did, (thereby breaking one of the hard limits—one of the major rules) they would not be welcomed in the Dominants household.

Remember, the Dominant/submissive relationship is based on trust! Once trust is broken or a betrayal occurs there is no foundation to work with, as the Dominant knows the submissive/slave is not trustworthy and would most likely be untrustworthy in the future. And yes, the trust is required of the Dominant as well. Though the slave/submissive does not dismiss the Dominant, the slave may choose to sever their contract and their ties with the Dominant.

Dismissal can also occur if the Dominant feels the slave is not meeting the Dominant's needs or the slave/submissive was not at a compatible level with them.

It is common practice for Dominants to request referrals from past Masters/Mistresses, or even fellow submissives, from a submissive/slave under consideration. Though ultimately it is the Dominant's decision whether or not to accept a slave, some Dominants will decide against accepting a slave based on the feedback provided. I find women more so than men will check on references and prior interactions and behavior patterns—both from a submissive or Dominant perspective.

Negotiations:

Negotiations are typically performed between two individuals who have recently met or are *Playing* for the first time. Negotiations determine what is allowed during a particular interaction and what is not. It should be noted that each *Scene/Play* carries its own negotiations and what was acceptable in a former scene together may not necessarily be acceptable in the current one. At anytime during the negotiation process one or both of the individuals may decide *Play* would not be acceptable for whatever reason, often because the Dominant wants to be able to do more than the submissive is offering, or visa versa.

A Mistress/Master who already owns a submissive/slave does not negotiate the *Scene/Play* with His/Her submissive/slave as submissive's hard limits have already been established by the Dominant and any interactions within those parameters is deemed acceptable. Often, once a submissive/slave is collared, his *hard limits* are those the Dominant has established for him and/or are the *hard limits* of the Dominant.

During negotiations, a *Safeword* is established and an individual's *soft* and *hard limits* are reviewed and agreed upon. Both the Dominant and submissive must agree to respect these during *Play*. Duration of *Play* is also established. For example, a time constraint can be in place—*Playing* for two hours or half an hour. Agreement over what implements will be used—for example, deciding between Floggers and Crops and Canes (or all of them) is reached. They also discuss techniques like Knife play and Bondage and how each activity will be performed. For instance, will the Spanking be performed with a hand, a belt, or a paddle? Remember, BDSM is all about the psychological connections made by the individuals internally or externally as couple. We'll discuss this further in a later chapter.

Though negotiations are typically made before engaging in actual *Play*, they can also be performed once *Play* has begun. For example, an interaction can begin with a restriction on only open-handed Spanking, but as the *Play* continues the Dominant or submissive may wish to agree on the stronger sensation of a paddle or hairbrush. Or maybe it was negotiated that a Whip would be used, but the submissive later requested to not have the Dominant continue using it.

Also it's important to realize that the individuals are constantly communicating throughout the interaction. For instance: the Dominant may be Flogging the slave and occasionally—purposely—flog between his legs striking the penis and scrotum. The slave would then advise the Dominant that the force is too strong as his recent vasectomy makes it hard for him to tolerate too much pressure in that area at this time. The Dominant then lightens *Her* strikes and/or moves to a different area of his body to torment.

Anything and everything can be negotiated including sexual contact and specific sexual acts. For instance, oral sex might be permissible but anal sex can be a *limit*. Or penetration can only be conducted with an adult sex toy and not with the other person's genitals. And of course, safe sex practices can be established and negotiated as well—something I always recommend if not in a closed relationship.

BDSM for Writers Checklist:

There are several wonderful books on the market and online which outline various Checklists you can use. Just for you, I have created a specific *BDSM Checklist* in this book which I believe will assist you when creating your characters and developing their characteristics as well as give you ideas on activities and interactions they can perform. You will also be able to identify which activities have specific emotional connections for your characters. It'll also be a great guide and resource tool to help you develop and/or play with the possibility of various erotic activities, punishments, corrections which your characters can engage in.

Typically it is the submissive who completes the *BDSM Checklist* and gives it to the Dominant for review. However, I always recommend the Dominant completes His/Her own list to help determine what their unconscious limits are and where their boundaries lie.

The *BDSM Checklist* is not a measurement of how kinky a person is. There is no judgment for being willing (or unwilling) to give or receive an activity. There is no good or bad. The *BDSM Checklist* merely helps an individual, especially the submissive, understand the vast possibilities in BDSM and, based on those answers, allows the Dominant to get a better grasp of where the submissive's needs, desires, even their fears lay.

For instance: Spanking is a pretty simple activity. However it has many variations and each variation is wrapped in its own emotional connections. Let me give you an example: a Spanking can be performed *Over the Knee*, which carries with it some sense of humiliation. Now imagine the level of humiliation which would occur if the person had to pull their pants and underwear down to their ankles then lay across the Dominant's lap? Spanking also varies greatly if a hair brush, belt, or shoe is used instead of merely an open palm. Though it's all the same activity—a Spanking—the actual emotional connections, whether conscious or unconscious, will greatly affect the interaction between the *giver* and the *receiver*, the Dominant and the submissive. (I provide a more in-depth psychological review on the benefits of the *BDSM Checklist* and the emotional intricacies it reveals in the chapter on *BDSM for Writers Checklist*).

It's imperative to remember that an individual's *BDSM Checklist*—those things he/she will and will not perform or adhere to—even enjoys and finds erotic—is constantly changing. This is why I always have a slave/submissive complete a new *BDSM Checklist* every six months to a year.

Changes occur over time and are due to a variety of reasons. They may occur because of the comfort level the submissive/slave develops with the individual they are interacting with and the desensitization of the negative emotions associated with a particular activity. They may occur merely because the submissive wants to push themselves farther. Perhaps he or she discovered that they tried something and didn't like it or realized they weren't emotionally ready to dabble in that area.

It's imperative to understand and accept that what the individual (your characters—either Dominant or submissive) may have found extremely erotic when fantasizing can turn out to be distasteful in reality. The changes can occur because the individual has worked through whatever issue it was that blocked acceptance of that aspect of themselves and/or their partner. It can even be as simple as being turned on by observing another individual participating in the activity. Regardless of the reason, just have your character mark it on the list as appropriate. Keep in mind that your characters preferences may change with their continued interactions or across a series.

Edge Play:

Edge Play is considered an advanced form of BDSM interaction which not all individuals in the lifestyle participate in. Though any aspect of BDSM involves physical and even emotional risks and/or consequences, *Edge Play* interactions are dangerous and can lead to serious injuries and/or emotional distress. In some rare cases, *Edge Play* can lead to unintentional death. I've listed a few examples of *Edge Play* below.

One of the more common forms of *Edge Play* is *Breath Play*, which is where you restrict a person's natural ability to breathe. Asphyxiation is another form of *Breath Play*, which involves actual strangulation. This is one of the higher levels of Edge Play and responsible for many accidental deaths; it is classified as autoerotic asphyxiation. This can be performed with a partner or alone.

Fire Play is where you use fire as an erotic interaction; this does not include candle wax. *Fire Play* is considered dangerous based on the possibility of second and third degree burns.

Knife Play is where a knife or straight razor is used to cut or simulate cutting on the body. There is also an even higher level of *Knife Play* where actual penetration of the vaginal, penal and anal cavity is performed. I do not endorse this activity due to its extreme level of risk; however as with anything else, this is a personal choice. I would strongly caution you about mentioning it in your novels, due to the extreme emotional reactions it can evoke from readers.

Fear Play incorporates anything the person fears, whether from a physical or emotional aspect, and can be used with or without actual physical interaction. *Fear Play* doesn't necessarily have to incorporate an individual's actual known fears. It can be any *play* that produces the sensation of fear to a higher degree. Note I am talking about fear not terror. You don't want the submissive so fearful they can't think or worse go into shock. Also, physically speaking, keeping the individual on the edge of fear will allow for hours of wicked fun; pushing them into terror you have about 15 to 30 minutes tops before their body and mind shuts down and they are incapacitated—sometimes less.

And of course, *Mind Fucks* are those deliciously sinful thrills which incorporate mental and physical interactions, pushing both the submissive/slave and Dominant to a higher emotional and mental level of interaction where reality is at times distorted and two contradictory truths co-exist simultaneously, causing confusion and distress. The goal isn't to cause an emotional breakdown but to push the slave to the edge. *The Forked Tongue* by Flagg is a must have book for authors who want to learn some of the intricacies which make a great *Mind Fuck* possible.

Humiliation Play:

The complexities and levels of *Humiliation Play* vary from a simple tease, to embarrassment, to outright degradation. This is an individual preference within the couple. Not everyone agrees with or participates in *Humiliation Play*. It's important to understand that *Humiliation Play* varies greatly and is vastly different for men than it is for women—not only from a physical perspective but an emotional and psychological one as well. What will trigger major reactions in a woman may be shrugged off by a man and vice-versa. We will discuss *Humiliation Play* from each perspective in greater detail in a later chapter as this is an entity in and of itself.

Aftercare:

No discussion on BDSM is complete without discussing *Aftercare*. Aftercare is as important to the BDSM community as foreplay is to the vanilla community. Aftercare is what happens once the *Scene* is over. Aftercare is often agreed upon during negotiations. It is typically the Dominant's responsibility to provide Aftercare for the submissive they interacted with or to make prior arrangements for it to be provided by another submissive or Dominant.

Aftercare can consist of holding the submissive/slave and reassuring him/her that they are still desired and accepted despite their behavior during the *Scene*. At times, depending on the intensity of the scene, the individual may feel a bit of embarrassment or shame or have an emotional cathartic breakthrough and need emotional support. Aftercare can be as simple as sitting with the slave for a while to ensure they are ok, especially if the submissive is just someone the Dominant is casually interacting with or spending a few hours with them.

Oftentimes, a Dominant will contact the submissive the following day to check in with him or her and ensure the slave is doing alright or establish a check-in timeframe for the submissive to contact the Dominant conveying they are alright and in good mental health. Aftercare varies greatly between those individuals who are just *Playing* or staring a new relationship and those that are in an established relationship. It may also vary depending on whether the submissive/slave is a man or a woman.

Typically, it is the submissive who receives the Aftercare; however a Dominant at times is also in need of it as well, whether it's a back massage after a long Flogging *Scene* or reassurance after having pushed their submissive further than the Dominant felt comfortable doing. Aftercare for the Dominant is something that should be negotiated at the beginning of a *Scene* if the individuals are not in a serious relationship.

Typically the Dominant is not provided service immediately after a *Scene* unless He or She has more than one submissive. This is not because the submissive/slave is not willing to do so, but that in most cases the slave/submissive is physically or emotionally exhausted and/or are in what is called *subspace.*

Subspace:

Subspace is an emotional and physical phenomena which occurs in the submissive/slave during physical and/or sexual interactions. It can also occur during service to their Master/Mistress. It is an altered state of being; a comfort and sense of acceptance and wellbeing that occurs when the submissive/slave has reached a psychical or mental release and/or orgasmic state. It is a sense of fulfilling their ultimate goal and/or connecting with themselves and their Master/Mistress on a higher plain. It is where they let go of all of life and societal rules and requirements and they achieve bliss.

Physically, *subspace* occurs when adrenaline and/or endorphins are running high in the slave/submissive's body and his level of cognition and/or coordination is not present. Physically, the person becomes "loopy" and seems drunk or under the influence. The Dominant will want to watch for enlarged pupils and slow responses or incoherent ones, as these are all signs of *subspace.* In some instances the slave may even lose his ability to stand or sit and may even faint.

This is when "Quick Release" cuffs are a godsend. Having a chair nearby is always a good idea.

Because of this physical and biological effect, it's imperative to ensure the submissive/slave is fully cognizant of his surroundings and is able to function as needed before allowing him or her to leave your sight or be left unattended. The slave/submissive should never be allowed to go home, especially if he's driving, unless fully cognizant. If necessary, get a reputable car service to take him home. It can take a few minutes to a few hours before the slave is fully cognizant, depending on the emotional and physical impact of the *Scene*.

There can be verbal, emotional, or physical triggers which place an individual into *subspace*. This can be anything from a word, a look, an instrument, even walking into a Dungeon or private Play room.

Sub-drop:

Sub-drop is where the submissive/slave experiences an emotional crash based on their interactions and surrender. At times, there is guilt and shame from his/her surrender and the activities he/she engaged in or the emotional connection he/she formed. The slave/submissive may become extremely emotional, agitated, or even teary during or after the interaction.

For instance, one submissive I knew began to cry as his Mistress was putting away their equipment after their *Scene*. He clung to her waist as he knelt before her "thanking her for taking care of him" during and after their *Play*. He stated it was the way she reassured him when he became scared and how she checked on his bonds that assured him she valued him and cared for him and that he had not felt that way in a long time.

It is not uncommon for a submissive to enjoy their BDSM interactions and a day or so later feel ashamed of those very desires and run away, refusing to speak to the Dominant or interact with *Him/Her* further. It is at these times that the submissive/slave needs the support of his/her peers and the reassurance of the Dominant, as the emotional and psychological upheaval can be devastating. The submissive may even undergo an emotional crisis based on who they believe themselves to be as compared to what they think their sexual desires implies they are. It can create a terrifying experience.

It is this internal struggle that may lead a submissive to accuse the Dominant of wrongdoing, which is a situation in which male Dominants may find themselves in hot water—like legal issues—and female Dominants may find themselves with a very aggressive and disrespectful male. Male submissives do not bring their complaints to the police because of social stigmas; however, if they did, more Dominant woman might find themselves needing legal representation and the services of NCSF (National Coalition for Sexual Freedom).

Also, it's imperative to remember and understand that we all have triggers from our pasts, traumatic experiences, and secret baggage that we may not have worked through. These very issues may arise from a simple BDSM interaction such as a Spanking or giving service (whether sexual or not) that was performed. This is why most conscientious Dominants will check in with the submissive the next day or within a few days after their interactions to ensure his/her mental well-being.

However, ultimately, it is the submissive's responsibility to discuss these experiences—*sub-drops*—with the Dominant and/or individuals he/she engages with, especially if the drops are severe, as no good Dominant/Master/Mistress would ever want to emotionally injury another human being. In this situation, it may be in the submissive's best interest to forego BDSM interactions for a while as they enter therapy to work on these emotionally devastating issues and become stronger.

Domspace/Top-space:

As opposed to *subspace* where the body is flooded with endorphins, *Domspace* is where the Dominant is flooded with adrenaline and the Master/Mistress may be "floating" in their own euphoric sense of well-being and satisfaction. It is not uncommon for the Dominant to experience a type of mental orgasm due to *His/Her* interactions with the slave/submissive. However whereas the slave is "loopy", the Dominant becomes hyper and full of energy. Some male Dominants may even achieve a mental/emotional climax without ejaculation. And of course, a female Dominant may achieve an emotional and/or physical orgasm without sexual interactions.

As with subspace, the feeling of total acceptance, completion and peace is also something the Dominant may experience; perhaps even a feeling of oneness with their slave/submissive.

Dom-drop

This is the term used for a Dominant who is experiencing a drop in *His/Her* emotions. Unlike Domspace/Top-space where the individual is experiencing an adrenaline rush and feeling euphoric and hyperactive, during *Dom-drop* the Dominant can experience an emotional drop based on the interactions he or she engaged in with the submissive/slave. These feelings can include: guilt, shame, fear, even moral questioning of themselves can arise.

Remember, it is the Dominant who is orchestrating the *Scene,* pushing the submissive/slave off the cliff; *He* or *She* is the one yielding the Whip—literally. These activities at times can cause an individual to question his or her sanity and character. In essence, they may ask themselves how they could have willingly hurt another individual, regardless of whether that person enjoyed it or not. (Remember hurt not injured!). The Dominant may degrade themselves for finding pleasure from engaging in such behavior—especially *Fear play* and *Edge Play,* activities which are much more intense. The Dominant may even punish themselves verbally for finding sexual release from having forced their partners to perform a degrading act; or for causing pain and madding their partner cry—especially a male partner. At times BDSM can make a Dominant question His/Her sanity, their morals, even their very essence—and it doesn't help that society portrays those that engage in these types of activities as mentally ill, criminal, or perverted in their desires. I find that Dominant women, more so than Dominant men, experience *Dom-drop* because of the standards and biases in our culture.

Here's an example of *Dom-drop*. A Dominant woman I knew had interacted with a new submissive who demanded she *Spank* him, begging her until she finally relented. The next day, he accused her of "violating" him because not only did she *Spank* him as he desired but she bit him as well. She was devastated, questioning herself and her behavior. It wasn't until another Dominant helped her put the submissive's behavior into perspective that she let go of the guilt she felt and realized it was the submissive's own feelings of shame and inadequacy that he was projecting onto her.

At times Dom-drop can occur if the Dominant feels they have crossed a line into questionable abusive behavior or the scene they participated in stirred up memories of past personal trauma. As with the submissive's *sub-drop,* working through these issues, discussing them with peers, or even addressing them with a kink friendly therapist will help the individual overcome the emotional impact and allow them to move forward and accept themselves fully once more—or at the very least be able to place the undesired emotions into a more acceptable perspective.

Polyamory:
Although not everyone in the BDSM community is into Polyamory, enough are for this topic to be discussed. Polyamory is a lifestyle in which you have more than one partner in any romantic and/or sexual relationship. In the BDSM community, Polyamory is not always sexual in nature. It can be merely service-oriented or based on other physical, non-sexual interactions.

The majority, if not all, Polyamorous groups are closed off to most outside individuals where sexual interactions are concerned; however, physical, non-sexual interactions with others are often permissible.

Polyamory has its own list of rules which are unique to each couple and/or group—each household has and makes its own. Enforcement of these rules is up to the ruling body and/or the Dominant in charge. Failure to abide by these rules can lead to *dismissal* of the individual from the group.

BDSM Household:
BDSM Households can be comprised of one or more Dominant/Master/Mistress and several slaves/submissives. Each slave and/or submissive will have a particular role within the Household structure. For instance, one slave may be used for sexual purposes, the other for household duties, and a third for professional or work-related duties. However, all the slaves/submissives will have one common duty—to see to the service and fulfillment of the Master's/Mistress' needs.

There are rules and protocols which each individual within the Household adheres to. Failure to do so can be disciplined with training, correction, or punishment, and in extreme cases, dismissal.

Each Household is unique. Often Dominants/Masters/Mistresses will gather together or attend workshops specifically designed to address any issues which develop and learn how to make their Households more efficient.

Munch:
A Munch is the equivalent of a potluck. Individuals gather together once a month (or more often if the group desires). During the Munch the individuals will mingle, get to know each other, or reacquaint themselves with friends they haven't seen since the last gathering. The Munch provides an opportunity to talk and enjoy a little conversation and even negotiate with someone you'd like to *Play* with. Most Munches are conducted in a neutral setting such as a Diner or other public location. After the Munch, those that are going to *Play* meet up at the designated home, *Play Space,* or BDSM club. Some individuals open their private dungeons or homes to the group after a Munch. I've even known a group that rents a hotel suite for the day and converts it into their own *Private Dungeon.*

Contracts:
Contracts outline in detail the terms by which a submissive/slave agrees to interact within the relationship and the terms he or she will abide by. It may also include the

protocols and rituals required by the Dominant. Some contracts are fairly simple, while others are elaborate. It is not uncommon for a Dominant/Master/Mistress to include a list of his or her responsibilities toward the slave/submissive and what they will provide to the slave/submissive in exchange for services rendered.

For example: the submissive/slave agrees to not date anyone else or interact sexually with another while under the contract; the submissive will make him/herself available twice a week on specific dates and times to meet with the Master/Mistress. The submissive will wear a certain type of uniform when in the Master's presence. The Master/Dominant in turn agrees to provide the submissive/slave with *His/Her* guidance and emotional support. The Master/Mistress agrees to take care of the submissive's sexual and physical/BDSM needs. The Dominant agrees to never abuse the submissive/slave in word or deed and to treat him/her with respect, all within the context of a BDSM relationship and for a specific length of time.

Some couples make up their own portion of the contract, aside from the basic terms, as a sort of "wedding vow" that outlines what they'd like to share with each other. It's very touching.

Most *Contracts* are one year in duration, a sort of probationary period like an engagement prior to entering into a more permanent relationship.

Though the *Contract* is not typically legal and would not withstand *vanilla* judgment and/or court enforcement, as no one can legally enslave themselves or another person, the *Contract* is viewed as a binding commitment for individuals in the BDSM community. Those who do not honor their *Contracts* are frowned upon regardless of the excuse given—unless, of course it was a matter of safety. Remember I mentioned the community is actually very close-knit and word gets around.

Contracts are sacred within the BDSM community equivalent to vanilla marriages, thus individuals do not enter into them lightly and are honor-bond to uphold them; however, some individuals do jump from collar to collar,

Dominant to Dominant. Within the community, we call these *Velcro collars* and they're seen as less significant submissives.

By virtue of the contract, the submissive technically becomes a slave taking him/her from being independent and being able to set limits, to being owned and having the limits imposed by the Master/Mistress as set forth in the contract. Therefore regardless of whether or not he/she is given that title to begin with or continues being called or thinking of themselves as a "*submissive*" in essence he/she is now a slave.

****

I can continue providing you with definitions; however, that would take up at least another forty pages. For now, the definitions I've touched upon are the most important aspects and fundamentals of BDSM. As you continue to explore and research, navigating your way through the erotic and emotional complexities of this amazingly diverse topic and lifestyle, remember that everyone's opinion varies based on his/her experience level, experiences, and perspective. What someone is comfortable doing today may have been an activity they were terrified to dabble in and share with another five years ago, or even six months ago. Thus, when conducting interviews with others for your research, ask the individual what it felt like when they were first learning about BDSM and what it is like for them now.

Never rely solely on the input of men and women whose only experiences are from online interactions, people who haven't experienced BDSM face-to-face with another, or those who've obtained all their experience from books or talking to friends. If they haven't actually experimented with and experienced BDSM for themselves, they can't really understand the vast complexities of this psychologically and emotionally rich lifestyle. (Neither can you, yet, if you're just starting out.) Nor could they possibly understand or have a true concept of the physical aspects of BDSM, though they can experience and share with you some of the emotional connections they've made. What they've experienced in their "virtual reality" fantasies is vastly different from the often indescribable physical and emotional connections formed in person. It doesn't matter how much research they have done, how many individuals they interviewed themselves, or how many books they've written—understanding the heart of BDSM and writing about it or discussing theory and your concept of it are two vastly different things. It's like being a male gynecologist—he may know the intricacies of a vagina, but he's never experienced a period, cramps, and the accompanying mood swings.

Take for instance the true story of Tom, a male Dominant who had been interacting with Betty over the internet for over eight months before they agreed to meet in person at a local BDSM club. During that time, Tom and Betty *Played* and interacted online four and five times a week. Assured of Betty's compliance and her desire to engage with him on a physical level, Tom tied her up in the public dungeon, caressed her, received her reassurance again and stepped back prepared to use a Single Tail Whip on her back; an activity they often engaged in virtually. On the first strike, Betty, the professed slave screamed, "Stop. Stop. It didn't hurt like this online!"

Need I say more?

As you research and explore, it's essential to remember—even to train yourself—to reserve your judgment and view the various activities and behaviors of BDSM with an open mind. It's imperative to understand that what you might find objectionable and offensive is quite the opposite for another individual. It is easy to pass judgment on a person or activity in this unique lifestyle when you do not understand the intricacies and emotions associated with it or the complex emotional and psychological connections made. You may even find yourself clinging to those popular beliefs and prejudices that Hollywood and our culture perpetuate about individuals in the BDSM lifestyle. Doing so is no different than passing judgment on another's sexual orientation or religious beliefs. I dare say BDSM today is discriminated against as much as the GLBT (Gay/lesbian/bi-sexual/transgender) community was discriminated against twenty and thirty years ago.

Make no mistake, BDSM is not merely a sexual erotic pleasure or something naughty to enjoy when you're bored with *vanilla* sex. For some it is a way of life and an intricate part of who they are, even if they do at times struggle with their own self-acceptance.

Though you may be writing "fantasy romance," as one author stated during a panel discussion, you are writing about a particular lifestyle and way of life: give it the reverence, or, at the very least, the respect it deserves.

Chapter 4

Psychology and Misconceptions

There is a common misconception that individuals who participate in BDSM activities whether as Dominant or submissive have a few screws loose. All too often from a psychological perspective they are immediately diagnosed as having some sort of pathology and perhaps sociopathic tendencies. This is far from the truth! And yet, in some ways—in some individuals—perhaps there is a little truth to it, especially since the line between pathology and eroticism is so thinly veiled. In fact, in several states BDSM activities are considered unlawful even when performed by consenting adults and some couples have been arrested because of it.

Have you ever wondered what these types of people look like?

Well, let me tell you. They look just like the men and women you see walking down the street or sitting on the bus or train beside you every day. He or she is your neighbor, your co-worker; dare I say, even the person sitting next to you at church. They are men and women such as yourself who have families and jobs, perhaps even children. They come from every economic and social background as well as religious, ethnic and sexual orientation. They have the same hopes and dreams you have of someday having a home, a loved one, and basically having a happy fulfilling life.

They might even be you!

I want to point out that an individual doesn't just wake up one morning with these desires. These desires have been with him or her since childhood. As John Money asserts, dominance and submission is their Love Map.

These mentally healthy men and women do not participate in BDSM activities because they wish to be abused nor do they desire to perpetuate malicious acts on another human being for a sexual thrill. Nor do they desire to hurt or injure someone who's put their faith, trust and even their very life in another's hands. They participate in these activities because it is what they've learned and find comfort and sexual satisfaction in. It is their Love Map, and yes, they are normal!

Hollywood and authors who do not understand the dynamics of this intensely erotic and diverse lifestyle have perverted (no pun intended) the fundamental truths of the BDSM lifestyle out of ignorance or for their own gains perpetuating misconceptions and myths which have lead to discrimination and bigotry toward participants; much as in decades past the same was perpetuated against Gays and Lesbians. And just as with the GLBT (gay, lesbian, bi-sexual, and transsexual) community, many BDSM lifestylers who are discriminated against have been fired from their jobs, become ostracized from their families, and some have even lost custody of their children.

Yes, there are criminals in our society who dominate their victims and do horrible sadistic things. Yes, there are individuals in relationships who manipulate their partners and abuse them. However, these abusive behaviors are not the foundation of *Dominance and submission*. Though these negative behaviors can be found in the BDSM community, they are more prevalent in the vanilla community.

It may surprise you to learn that the majority of the men and women who participate in BDSM activities and embrace Dominance and submission as well as Master/slave relationships are honorable people who communicate their boundaries and learn how to engage in healthy relationships through various workshops and interactions. Unfortunately as with any other community, we tend to notice the bad apples first and this taints the way for the rest.

Though I would love to paint a wonderful picture of honorable men and women and portray individuals who just want to be free to love and express their inner libertarianism, the truth is there are many individuals—both men and women—who enter the BDSM community for the wrong reasons. Some use it as a way to exorcize their childhood and adult demons; to feel powerful because in their vanilla life they don't; and sadly, to be "abused" because they're so broken from their past life experiences that they try to find a way to recreate those past traumatic experiences. Regrettably, instead of going to therapy where they belong and can begin the healing process, these individuals turn to BDSM. The reasons vary greatly from individual to individual.

As for those who use BDSM as a spiritual or self-actualization path, they too find their own delicate balance within service and the vast array of *power exchange* activities.

It's paramount to understand that BDSM is not merely about sexual conquests or interactions. It is about so much more! Some relationships do not incorporate sexual activities at all and are merely focused on various aspects of service or Dominance and submission. At times the relationships involve a spiritual connection, at others an emotional or physical one. Sometimes the connection is in the form of mentorship and acceptance, not only from the dominant but from the slave as well. These roles are forever intertwining, blurring, and readjusting as each individual receives what they need from the relationship and grows in a positive way from it—if it is a healthy relationship.

"When the purpose of the interaction is not just orgasm but another kind of release as well, one moves to a deeper level of relationship that is more sophisticated and requires more thought and communication."

A slave boy I know shared with me the passage above which I believe puts into perspective the essence of BDSM.

Before I talk about the "*Frogs* in the Pond"—those individuals who enter the community for all the wrong reasons—I'd like to introduce you to the four primary types of mentalities that comprise the community. These unique individuals who carry themselves with dignity and honor and respect the rights of those around them and those they interact with.

<u>The Dominant:</u>
He or She desires to establish a connection with an individual who is willing to give and share of themselves completely. The Dominant seeks someone who is willing to

follow directions and be guided even when the submissive/slave doesn't concur with the decisions made. The Dominant seeks a man or woman who will be there to share their essence and embrace the life the Dominant is trying to build. At their core, the Dominants crave to share the true essence of themselves, their desires, and their eroticism with someone who will cherish these gifts and offer their surrender in return. As with any other relationship, the Dominant may desire to merely brush along the surface and delve into basic levels of BDSM going no further.

The Master/Mistress:

Though they embody the characteristics of the Dominant, this individual will take the relationship one step further into an emotionally and physically intense level of connection which is not merely about "playing and satisfying desires. This individual, whether man or woman, will explore the full spectrum of possibilities, opening the door to growth not only for the submissive/slave but for themselves as well. The Master has a willingness to teach, share, and experience Eros and Thanatos (the dark shadow of desire) with another and balance the two halves of their soul. The Master's intention is not to harm but to enlighten; to accept another's vulnerabilities and teach the submissive/slave the power he/she holds within, since a slave that has poor self-esteem doesn't serve the Master nor themselves to their full potential.

Imagine a relationship based on trust and acceptance that is continuously affirmed; this is what the Master/Mistress strives to achieve.

The submissive:

The submissive desires to be of use to the Dominant trusting his or her gift of submission will not be abused. He or she longs to share that part of themselves they've hidden from the rest of the world. Their need to be of service, to take care of another, to surrender themselves completely sexually, physically, emotionally, to make their Master's/Mistress' life easier as that brings the submissive joy and actually fortifies them and gives them the strength to battle life's challenges.

Though the submissive tends to have a beta personality, he or she can be very domineering in their own way and often chooses to surrender to only one other individual— their Master.

The slave:

As these men and women make the transition from submissive to slave, they relinquish their ego and societal norms to surrender themselves unconditionally to their Master/Mistress allowing the Dominant to take the lead and rebuild or re-design their lives in a more positive venue, knowing that surrendering completely to their vulnerability and handing it over to their Master/Mistress will bring with it only affection and acceptance unlike in many vanilla interactions where such behavior would be seen as a weakness.

There is an old saying in the community that it takes more strength and courage to kneel than it does to stand— and the slave embraces this concept. It is through their complete surrender that they find the essence of themselves and can then share it with another and the world at large in a multitude of ways. It may surprise you to know that often very powerful men, like doctors, wall street executives, even special forces soldiers are among the most submissive and/or *sexual submissive* men there are.

Regrettably over the years I've noticed that many *submissive women* who seek a Dominant man within the vanilla community actually find an abuser instead. It's a shame that these women don't realize that it is the above description of the Master above that they seek and perhaps if society wasn't so bias against sexual freedom these women would know where to look. Unfortunately, women aren't the only ones who find an "abuser" when searching for a dominant partner, male submissives experience this as well.

***

Now let's talk about the *Frogs*—the wannabes, as they're called within the community, who create frustration and discourse. Unfortunately their numbers are so staggeringly high they actually seem to have touched the lives of everyone in the community at one time or another. Just as with the vanilla community, *Frogs* feel they're entitled to behave as poorly as they wish. Please note that each example below can be attributed to both men and women though I've stated the behaviors under the gender which I've observed it was most prevalent in.

From the Dominant perspective

In Men

These men have prior relationship issues and somewhat abusive personality as well as personal abuse issues that they're dealing with. They feel women should cater to them and are very derogatory toward her (whether she is Dominant or submissive). Misogyny is their motto. They look down upon the submissives (both male and female) who offer their vulnerability and feel entitled to a level of trust they have not earned. These *Frogs* (as I call them) often push their agendas making the submissive feel guilt or shame for not offering enough of themselves. These *Frogs* may secretly despise the submissive for their ability to surrender despite the *Frog's* own need to control them, which can spark emotional abuse in the guise of do.minance. These men will attempt to control Dominant women and when they can't or their advances are thwarted they become petty or disrespectful. These men can be very charismatic and lure the unsuspecting or new submissive to them only to blame the submissive for his own failures and shortcomings. These males are the wife abusers who enter the BDSM community in hopes of hiding their nature in the guise of dominance and sadomasochistic practices. Unfortunately, as mentioned before, many submissive women find these abusers and struggle with their desires to please and surrender not seeing the warning signs in time.

Many married men play in the BDSM community figuring their wives/partner will never learn of it because they don't allocate the same value to BDSM interactions or they do not interact with the slave/submissive sexually thus they do not view their interactions as cheating.

In Women

Some women—female *Frogs*—enter the community wanting to take out their frustrations on men for prior wrongs they've endured. These abusive women tend to treat submissive men like garbage and often require financial favors or "presents" from them. These types of women degrade the essence of a Dominant Women and create a bad reputation for all especially because any monetary requirement pushes the envelope of "financial prostitution". Don't misunderstand me, everyone loves getting gifts; however, there's a major difference between a man bringing you flowers and candy when coming to your home on the first few dates and one being required to pay you a set amount of money to "prove" his submissive is sincere. Though some men desire *financial dominance*, in this case, the requirement is "forced" and stems from a negative and selfish desire.

In Both men and women:

These *Frogs*—both men and women—may remain within the community standards of SSC (Safe, Sane, and Consensual) though they will push the envelope into sadistic practices as they ride the fine line of *consensual non-consensuality*. Though the majority of honorable Sadists in the community thrive on this line of *consensual non-consensuality*, the difference between a *Frog* and a sincere Sadist is that at the core of a ***healthy Sadist*** there is no malice; whereas within these *Frogs*, their malicious intent simply has not yet revealed itself or is in disguise. These *Frogs* typically feel powerless in their vanilla lives and use BDSM to appease that feeling of helplessness and vulnerability that they have hidden at their core.

You will often hear these *Frogs* speak of D/s as a "role" they "play", often compartmentalizing their vanilla and BDSM activities and refusing to interact with another BDSM practioners (even their own submissive) in the vanilla realm. These individuals are often married and troll the BDSM community in order to appease their unmet sexual desire.

These *Frogs* also tend to be extremely rigid with their rules and protocols and believe their way is the only correct way despite more experienced individuals trying to enlighten them.

From the submissive perspective

In men

Some men especially married ones and those in committed relationships, think BDSM is a wonderful way to get their kinky needs met and they figure they'll never be caught because their wife/partner/girlfriend would never wander into a Dungeon. Plus they figure no one from the D/s community would *out* him because they'd have to *out* themselves.

Sexually, these males want to engage the Dominant in some kink, often because sex with their girlfriends or wives is boring. These *Frogs* figure that if they join a *Dominant Women's Group* or a kinky website, they'll find a woman, pretend they want a relationship, and get a "free play session" from the Dominant woman, instead of finding and paying a professional Dominatrix for her services. These *Frogs* make it hard for the sincere submissive who is serious about interacting with a Dominant woman as many have become jaded and distrustful of his honest gift due to past experiences.

In Women

As for submissive women who enter the community for the wrong reasons, they tend to use it as a therapy session, working out their problems with authority or with abuse and bad relationships hoping they'll find a Dominant man or woman who'll protect them and make all the decisions for them, demanding they be allowed to relinquish all their responsibilities—thus, creating a situation in which the Dominant will take the fall when things go wrong.

These submissive women, who would be better off addressing their problems in therapy, become very demanding and clingy and require massive amounts of reassurance. They will immediately label anything and everything the Dominant does that they don't approve of as "abusive". These women create their own rules as they go along and blame everyone else for their own mistakes. They hop from one Dominant to another to another in search of the "perfect one" who will meet her needs and make all their dreams come true. Often these female *frogs* will be accused of *Topping from the bottom* as they attempt to control the actions of their Dominant. (*Topping from the bottom* is where the submissive tries to control and dictate the scene and what is done to them, instead of letting the Dominant retain control.)

In both submissive men and women:

Another trait that immediately identifies these *Frogs* is their insistence that the Dominant set all the rules, thus taking no responsibility whatsoever for their submission or for the relationship itself. Whereas a slave or submissive will offer their will and their vulnerability to their Master/Mistress because they desire to serve at that intense level of connection and commitment, these *Frogs* merely want the ability to be as "bad" as they can get away with in a relationship then accuse the Dominant of not being able to "control" them.

There are even submissives who enter into a BDSM relationship or merely *Play* with a Dominant taking more punishment or physical pain than they are able to because they crave the *Aftercare* that will follow. These extremely damaged and abused individuals would do better in therapy but refuse to address their issues head on or hide from the need of the same. These damaged individuals will experience a 20 minute Flogging scene and require an hour plus of *Aftercare*. They may even demand it in specific ways or deem the Dominant "abusive" if they didn't receive their "punishment" or their Aftercare precisely the way they demanded. These individuals are very toxic for the Dominant as well as themselves!

71

***

The essential thing to remember about the BDSM lifestyle is that it is exactly like any other community around. It has its good apples and bad seeds. The only difference here is that coming across a bad seed can literally get you injured or killed. These are the reasons why the D/s community tends to *police* itself since anything bad that happens reflects poorly on the rest of the community as a whole.

Chapter 5

Personality Traits
&
Character Development

The most important essence of any novel is its characters and the credibility of their personalities. Nowhere is this fact more essential than in a BDSM romance. Though you can get away with sprinkling an array of traits you desire most in your characters and have them behave and interact with others in any given situation as you wish (after all, it is fiction), in a BDSM novel your characters must incorporate certain traits which are specific to their identifying role in order for them to be credible. Even if your readers are not knowledgeable about the intricacies of the BDSM lifestyle, they would likely immediately spot traits which were not congruent with your character's identity. Never forget that even those who aren't privy to the dynamics of a Dominance and submission relationship have seen enough movies or TV shows to have some concepts of the characteristic traits of a Dominant and a submissive. These inconsistencies would leave them wondering about your reliability as an author and might actually have them bypass your other novels even if you're otherwise a great story teller.

I recall reading a novel by an author who had a four book series. I love following series where the women are strong and tough. At the very beginning of the book I enjoyed the characters and the storyline. However, as I began reading chapter three I was so appalled by the unrealistic actions of her heroine (a government special agent, who stopped to answer her girlfriend's phone call during a shoot out.) The heroine even apologized because she had to "hang up". Call me cynical, but any one, man or woman, who stops to have a casual chat while in such a dangerous situation is just plain stupid. And that's not a character I care to read about. Needless to say, I haven't taken the chance on any of her other books.

As you already know readers are fickle! You want to capture their interest and have them come back for more. You want to create loyal readers who will not only purchase your books but tell all their friends about them. So let's talk about how you can create believable BDSM characters so they'll do just that.

Below is a breakdown of the primary characters in any D/s relationship. Hopefully these helpful hints into their personality traits will assist you in creating credible Dominant and submissive characters as you write your next novel. I've also included a few examples of what these character traits actually look like. I've used my own personal preference of the Dominant woman and male submissive for my examples however these genders roles are interchangeable. Though I've provided some gender specific examples as well, I won't be able to cover them all; however, you will get the general idea. As the meticulous writer I'm sure you are, I've no doubt you'll also do some additional research into character traits and the BDSM lifestyle as well.

The Dominant/Sadist Perspective:

According to many in the psychological community sadomasochistic behavior is still considered pathological and it is in the Diagnostic and Statistical Manual (DSM)—the psychologists reference guide to psychological disorders—as such. The DSM did ease up a bit by saying the behavior is only pathological if it creates emotional discomfort and undue stress to the individual; or if the activities are non-consensual in nature. I have to chuckle at that clause since many men and women who embrace the BDSM lifestyle struggle with their desires and the way they contradict societal norms and the prejudices they've been taught.

It's expected that in 2013, the psychological community in charge of creating the new DSM-5 will change the current mental illness diagnosis of sadists, masochists, fetishists and transvestic fetishists into a "non-disordered paraphilias". Thus being Kinky will no longer be a mental disorder. We have the National Coalition for Sexual Freedom (NCSF) to thank for their efforts in this regard and working to safeguard our sexual freedom.

Legally, the acceptance of consensual sadomasochism is different in every state. In some states, even consensual BDSM is a crime. Thus, every person should learn what's true for their state as ignorance of the law is not an excuse, and it can get you thrown in jail.

Another specific type of Dominant role is the Daddy and Mommy. Note that though they may refer to their submissives as "little boys and girls", their partners *are in fact adults*.

Daddy and Mommy Dominants bring their own unique behaviors and psychological connections to the BDSM table. Though they may be Sadistic and sexual with their *little girls* and *boys* depending on the role playing age, their approach to dominance is often based on guidance and mentorship. Daddy and Mommy Dominants can be more affectionate or more strict depending on the behavior of the *"child"*.

Please remember that when I mentioned *little girls* and *boys* I am specifically referring to those men and women who are of **legal age** and enjoy role playing NOT chronological minors. These adult age playing individuals open their imaginations and hearts and fulfill that essence of themselves that they didn't get to interact with during their childhood or that they just want to share and explore more of with someone they trust to guide them and keep them safe.

Unlike popular misconceptions perpetuated by bad BDSM movies and books, Dominants aren't the unfeeling emotionally distant bastards who greedily demand tremendous feats of submission only to neglect their submissive's efforts of service and toss a few gratuitous comments of appreciation here and there. Neither do they yell and scream at their submissives to get them motivated like the drill sergeants in the old war movies. If you stop to think about it, anyone who has to yell and scream is actually showing a lack of control!

In the D/s realm, lack of control indicates inability to take command of a situation and doesn't encourage a submissive's trust or confidence. Typically only an inexperienced submissive would accept such behavior from their Dominant unless yelling and screaming was actually "part of" a scene they were specifically engaged in and/or forms of play they created together.

Another misconception is the idea that a confident Dominant would circle around trying to pick up a submissive jumping from one to the other at a gathering hoping someone would play with them. Yes, I have seen several men and women do this, however it is seen as pathetic by the community. One male Dominant I've seen always dragged his little bag of toys back and forth (on rollers) hoping to find someone to play with on any given club night. The really sad part about his was he looked so needy and pathetic no one ever took him seriously. Some *Frog* Dominants, typically males, will circle like a shark waiting for a newbie they can spank—someone who doesn't yet know any better.

Then there are the confident Dominants who carry on their conversations with friends keeping an eye out for submissives of quality observing them from afar and nodding to them in acknowledgement, then letting the submissive come to them. This confident Dominant would complete their conversation, then either call the submissive to them, or continue observing the submissive quietly, taking their measure and awaiting another day to approach them.

Another comical and common misconception is that every Dominant wants the submissive/slave to kneel before them before the submissive is allowed to speak to them. Personally, I hate when an unknown submissive kneels before me without permission. First, because if I didn't notice he was kneeling, I'd probably trip over him. And secondly, if he's kneeling before me without even knowing me than that tells me he'll kneel for anyone. I desire a slave who values his surrender and submission more highly than that. Several Dominants I know feel the same; though not all Dominants view it that way and many enjoy when the submissive kneels before them in greeting. Like anything else in this lifestyle, it's all a matter of taste and the value you place on actions or lack thereof.

It should be understood that not all interactions with a Dominant will be physical and definitely not all will be sexual in nature. Some Dominants are interested in submissives merely for their ability to provide good service such as performing household chores, running errands, providing service in the form of accounting or other specialized skills. It is the service that then becomes the bases of the interaction between these two individuals.

Rewards for a good submissive may come in the form of acceptance and/or praise. One submissive I know loves to be able to cross-dress while providing service and be accepted for who he is. For him, being able to cook and serve a meal in a dress and heels allows him to be able to integrate that part of himself that he hides from the world. Imagine for a moment if you will what it feels like to be completely accepted for who you are. Finding one person who will not judge you or ridicule you, is invaluable.

My favorite misunderstanding is the belief that you have to dress in leather or a slinky outfit in order to dominate another. The truth is, if you can't dominate a person in fufu slippers, jeans, and a tee-shirt with no make-up on, you couldn't dominate them looking flawless in full leather regalia. Though you my look better in leather, it doesn't immediately give you *Super Dominant Powers* or a burst of confidence. Nor does the leather help improve your skills at Flogging or throwing a Whip. Not to mention, cheap leather squeaks and good leather is really expensive!

And just for the record, throwing a Whip around in three-inch heels is a pain in the ass (let alone four or five inch heels) especially when you bend down low to crack it against the slave's buttocks or back of his thighs and calves. Have you ever bent low in heels--not from the waist but actually bending your knees and going low--then tried to get up again without wobbling or worse yet, falling over? Imagine bending low repeatedly as you caress your slave's body with the Whip or a Flogger.

No one stands in one place with perfect balance when using any BDSM Toy. That would be like trying to kiss without moving your lips. And though we can all run in heels every now and then, a good scene can last anywhere from 30 minutes to a few hours—heels will kill your feet by the end of play—and may even cause you to cut it shorter than you intended.

I don't know about you, but I refuse to wobble about in heels. I value foot comfort. Yet even more than that, imagine how stupid you'd feel if you tipped over and fell on your butt while trying to Whip someone—especially if it happened in public.

As for female slaves, they do look great in heels. In their case however, the restraints they're placed in helps with their balance and besides, they're often hopping from one foot to the other or leaning forward on their toes. Not to mention the endorphins running through their body helps alleviate any immediate pain the shoes may cause. Yet mainly it's just that they're focused on other things going on and demands placed on them and don't necessary have time for their foot woos. However, their feet will definitely ache the next morning, along with a few other places.

One Dominant man I met actually took his slave's comfort into consideration so greatly that he purchased a pair of cowboy heel thigh high boots for her to wear, as opposed to the four -inch spiked ones most male Dominants prefer. When questioned by another male Dominant about it, he stated he valued his slave and planned to have her restrained for long periods of time thus wanted her as comfortable as possible so she'd "last longer" during their play.

Contrary to the myth that Dominants will accept any slave that darkens their doorway, or kneels before them, this is far from the truth!

Surprisingly, many male submissives—especially those new to the lifestyle—feel a female Dominant should immediately accept their surrender and actually become upset or belligerent when rejected even when the rejection is done respectfully. The male ego is the same in the BDSM lifestyle as in the vanilla realm!

As I previously mentioned, some males go to fetish clubs hoping to obtain a "free" Dominatrix session. You can easily spot these guys (and gals too). They're the guys that will go up to a group of women ask if they're dominant, and whether anyone wants to *spank* him. Kind of like the guy that goes to a table at a dance club and asks one woman after another to dance until he's rejected by all of them. Remember Dominants are selective and Master's are beyond discerning as a lot of work goes into training a submissive and guiding them into the slave you desire. I don't want to say men are the only ones guilty of such behavior as some female submissives behave just as poorly; however, I have experienced more men acting this way.

It's important to notice the tone of voice the Dominant uses and when. A stern voice can be used to reprimand a disobedient slave. There's no yelling and screaming involved just a very firm tone. Some Dominants use a softer more pleasant—even sensual—tone with their submissives luring them into their powerful web. In fact, it's the softer tone a Sadist takes with a submissive that scares them the most as the slave realizes that with a Sadist, it is when the Sadist is most quiet and thoughtful that they are creating the most physically torturous scenarios, calmly reaching for and embracing that sadistic side of themselves that they normally keep tightly leashed.

A major psychological difference between a Sadist and a Dominant is the fact that Sadists are turned on by inflicting physical pain and mental stressors, much more so than a Dominant and thus taking interactions to a higher emotional and physical level of torment. And though most Dominants enjoy inflicting some levels of pain on their submissives or slaves, whether through use of a Flogger, a Spanking, a Whip or hundreds of various toys, Sadists create an painful and/or psychological intensity that would make your typical Dominant cautious. It is the sadism itself which creates a sense of *rightness* and *peace* within the Sadist's mind and body.

Much like the submissive that experiences a rush of endorphins as their body registers pain, a Sadist will experience a rush of adrenaline which heightens their desire. Thus a Sadist engaging with a masochist creates a synergistic symbiotic connection between them wherein each receives what they desire. No, the slave doesn't necessarily have to be a masochist, the slave/submissive may simply accept the intensity because of their desire to please the Sadist.

I've known Masters/Mistresses who have stopped themselves from crossing the line with their submissive as they worked themselves up into a state of excitement that would push them into an area where their submissive would be taxed too highly either physically or mentally; thus, keeping the slave safe. And whereas the submissive will crash into *subspace* and become *pliant* due to all the endorphins running through their body, the Sadistic Dominant will become hyper and hit *Top-Space* due to all the adrenaline flooding theirs.

Some women experience a certain level of angst when embracing their Dominant or Sadistic side and may need some time and encouragement to embrace that aspect o themselves fully. It's not surprising really when we consider women are generally taught to be the "weaker sex" and not to assert themselves. They're seen as the bossy bitch that's on a power trip in the vanilla world when they behave as men are "allowed" to. Thus it's no wonder that when a woman first enters the lifestyle she may often feel guilt, even shame, for her desire to dominate others. And for a Sadistic woman, she may even fear herself as she embraces those darker more animalistic *Thanatos* desires within herself.

For Latina woman, there's also a cultural bias to struggle against as machismo is spoon feed into them from birth. The Latina will also struggle with religious beliefs which conflict with her desires. The Dominant Latina will stand apart from other Latinas who are submissive in nature. The Dominant Latina is a rarity—and the Sadistic one even more so.

Non-lifestyle friends will often accuse a Dominant woman of trying to emasculate her man or they will try to make her feel less than feminine and lacking in womanly virtues. This can make a Dominant/Sadistic woman feel isolated and cause her to turn against her very nature, hiding her desires from others even from herself—keeping a tight leash on her desires. She may even fear she's "abnormal" or pathological and perhaps even dangerous to others. This feeling of isolation creates an internal struggle that is felt by many Dominant women until they find the acceptance of the BDSM community or like-minded individuals.

A Dominant woman may often experience a power struggle within her relationships and/or experience a constant "serial dating" pattern as she shuffles from one lover to another trying to find what she desires; and more importantly, a partner who will not be *threatened* by her dominance and assertive ways. This behavior is most often seen in women who haven't made the cross over into the BDSM realm or who don't see their actions as "dominant" in nature. They tend to date other dominant personalities looking for an "equal" relationship when what they really seek is an alpha submissive or a sexual submissive.

Male Dominants don't seem to struggle with their dominant natures as much as it's a societal norm and to some extent it's acceptable for them to be aggressive and assertive. However, they may still struggle with their sadistic or domineering desires as society still views BDSM as a pathological affliction.

Punishment:

One thing almost every Dominant will agree upon is the fact that you don't touch a slave/submissive when you are angry. Doing so would be akin to abuse and the D/s and Master/slave relationships are based on mutual respect and even affection. Thus most Masters/Mistress' will dismiss their slaves for the night or send them to a corner while the Dominant cools off. Any punishment the submissive deserved will be decided and implemented when the Dominant has them self once more under control.

I knew a Sadist who purposely dropped her Crop onto the floor as she reined in her anger and stepped away from her slave to avoid causing him injury. She then sat and watched him hang from the ceiling for over an hour. The slave was devastated for having caused his Master such "pain" that he cried silently fearing she would *dismiss* him. As I've mentioned, the emotional bonds in these relationships are phenomenal.

Unfortunately for the submissive, this "time-out" allows the Dominant to reign in their tempers and carefully calculate the punishment, determining the level of severity— including the level of pain which will be inflicted. For example, where the submissive typically receives a hard Spanking during play time, this Spanking may leave welts or even draw blood from a Caning causing major discomfort for days.

In the end, it's all about the character of the individual and his or her honor. A person who cannot be trusted in everyday situations and who has no control over their temper is not a Dominant to be trusted or played with as their unpredictability makes them a risk to the submissive. It is why playing with a new Dominant for the first few times should always be done in public or after having thoroughly vetted the person (contacting their references and inquiring about the individual from other members of the community that you trust). Though not all individuals who are in the lifestyle engage in community events or are associated with public BDSM activities, those Dominants/Sadists who want to engage in higher levels of risk and *Edge Play* who refuse to learn how to keep their submissive safe aren't worth interacting with.

On a side note, it may also surprise you to learn that many Dominants (and submissives) will learn basic First Aid and CPR to ensure the safety of their partner.

When developing your character, you'll want to incorporate some of the traits above as well as use what the Dominant likes and how she/he identifies as a way to not only build erotic scenes but also their personality. Use the *BDSM for Writers Checklist* I've created to help you identify their desires and help you further categorize them and determine whether he or she is a Sadist, Daddy/Mommy Dom or merely a Dominant who enjoys service. You'll discover this immediately as you review the *BDSM for Writers Checklist* you've completed. If you've attributed more of the *Edge Play* scenarios to your character, make sure you've actually given them the experience and confidence to carry it off.

Despite the fact that most Sadists are good Dominants, it's perfectly acceptable if you provide your villainous character(s) with more sadistic tendencies; after all, they are the bad guys. Though wouldn't it be an interesting plot twist if two of your characters—the villain and the hero—had the same desires and playing patterns? What a thrilling BDSM suspense novel that would be.

As I mentioned above, the internal struggle a Dominant experiences at times with their own desires—especially sadistic ones—where they fear releasing the *"beast"* within and not being confident enough with themselves to be able to keep control of it will generate a wonderful storyline and/or great conflict within the book—especially if you have an experienced submissive/masochist who falls for an inexperienced or traumatized Dominant. This struggle is not only a great character identifier but also something you can use for/or against the Dominant as you develop his/her character and interactions with others since some people may see the *"Beast"* within the Dominant and others never get that privilege.

The submissive/slave Perspective:
There's a popular saying in the BDSM community that it's harder to kneel than it is to stand and it takes more courage to be vulnerable than it does to control another. This is never more true than with a male submissive who is going against societal norms by surrendering to another—especially to a woman. He is often viewed as less masculine or macho and the Dominant woman is accused of emasculating him. Yet, nothing is further from the truth!

In actuality, a submissive man can be more dangerous than a dominant one especially when his Mistress/Master is threatened. Think of him as the knight who goes off to battle and destroys his enemies than returning to meekly kneel before his Lady. This submissive male doesn't stop being a macho man; he embraces all aspects of his nature, making him stronger.

It is the fear of being ostracized by other men and the fear of embracing their desire for submission that leads most men to identify as Dominant when first entering the BDSM community—until they feel comfortable enough within the community and with themselves that they can then let go of their need to hide behind the façade of the Dominant male.

It is unfortunate that the submissive man's courage is often despised or openly ridiculed by Dominant men who make no qualms about putting down submissive man or showing their disdain. However these same Dominant men think nothing wrong with a woman being submissive. I believe this duality is caused by the Dominant man's own internal fear of being seen as weak, a fear and perhaps prejudice that keeps him from offering his own submission. And it's not unheard of for a *Dominant man* to swear a Dominant woman to secrecy about his desire to be submissive to "just her" and only "in private".

For some slaves, the ability to serve is what brings peace to their lives. It is the feeling of total acceptance and acknowledgement they strive to gain in their lives. They love to show their appreciation and respect by working hard to be a good slave and attempt to anticipate the needs of their Master/Mistress. These slaves even correct their own behavior before it needs to be addressed or punished. These types of slaves are a treasure to have and are well guarded once found.

As for submissive women, they're able to embrace the more feminine side of their nature as well as their desires to cater to their Dominant/Master/Mistress. She is able to give freely of herself knowing her efforts and service will be greatly appreciated. In this era when feminist ideals often battle with submissive desires, a female submissive/slave may find herself ostracized by her feminist friends for what they perceive as her *subservient* or *backward* desires or she may receive a lot of undue objections for being of service to her Dominant as she dutifully performs her tasks of being the attentive "wife" and/or partner. Of course, men also fall prey to these objections from their friends who will deem him "whipped". If they only knew how true it was!

Though the outside world may think a submissive suffers from little to no self-esteem or have a lack of personal power, the truth is far from it. In a way, submissive individuals are actually reclaiming their power and sharing it with others.

To dispel some rampant misconceptions, no slave/submissive is a doormat! Many are very strong, even dominant in their everyday vanilla interactions. Many have jobs where they are in charge or supervise others. They simply enjoy the ability to release their responsibilities and surrender to another individual they feel safe with.

The need for surrender is strong in both men and women and though not all interactions with their dominant are sexual in nature, I find that submissive women are used sexually more so than their male counterparts. This may be due to the physical dominance a woman excerpts over a man ensuring that he realizes that even his manhood *belongs to Her* and She'll use it when and as She desires. Also where male Dominants tend to be more comfortable being sexual in public, female Dominants often limit sexual interactions in public.

There's also a major difference between what a submissive/slave will engage in publicly versus private play. For instance, I've seen a male submissive withstand extreme physical torment in a public setting, including being Whipped and having Fire Play and Knife Play performed on him while he was restrained. Yet, this same individual had a major panic attack during private play alone with his Mistress when all that was done to him was placing him in cuffs—something she had done to him numerous times in the past. The fear behind the panic attack was caused by the fact that in public he could cry out for help any time he choose to and the Dungeon Master would intervene; whereas in private, there was no one to come to his rescue.

As for sexual play, many female Dominants will save the more intimate aspects of their interactions with their partner for private times. This is not only due to their personal preferences but because having to get in and out of their more elaborate outfits is a bit more difficult. With submissive women, it's not uncommon and perfectly normal for them to be seen in the nude and be forced to orgasm in public or perform fellatio on their Dominant in public.

For sexual submissives, their desire to serve and be vulnerable is based solely on their sexual needs and that is where their submission ends as in all other aspects of their lives and their interactions with their Dominant they are on equal footing and may even be dominant themselves. At times, you will have two Dominants who interact with each other successfully, outside the bedroom, because of the fact that one is a sexual submissive and therefore can give that aspect of themselves to the other. Though you may find that in these types of relationships, the couple may engage a third party they share as the submissive to one or both of them.

Submissives adhere to the requirements of their Dominant! Every Dominant has their own requirements and protocols. Some will impose eye contact restrictions; prescribe a dress code, as well as specific protocols and rituals dictating how the submissive will greet them when arriving for a *Play Scene* or when they meet up at home, if they live together. These rituals and protocols reinforce the connection between the couples and are paramount to the relationship. They provide a sense of belonging and acceptance, even safety, for both.

For those submissives that are masochistic in nature, you may find that they tend to push and challenge their Dominants to receive more physical interactions, even punishments. This push may not even be a conscious behavior on their part. However it is their physical, emotional and even spiritual need to connect at that level of release and service to their Dominant that pushes them to tease and bring forth the *Beast* within their Dominant.

A masochist whose needs aren't being met will often act out becoming rude, even disrespectful in hopes of being corrected and punished for his behavior. Unlike the slave who is in the relationship to be of service to his/her Dominant, the masochist can sometimes fall into the trap of being in service more for himself than to meet his Dominant's needs. For instance, being able to coax the sadistic aspects of his Dominant's nature is what he longs for, if he cannot, he will need another avenue to meet his desires. If he's in love with his Dominant and the Dominant isn't sadistic, the relationship may end or they will need to find a friend who is willing to serve their needs and inflict the sadism the slave/submissive craves.

For some masochist it's not so much that he's pitting himself against his Dominant, in the sense of taking as much as the Sadist/Dominant can provide, but pushing against his own fears or needs to be able to take more pain for his Dominant or himself needing to be pushed to extremes and know he's safe and will be cared for afterward. It is when the slave is pushed to these extremes that the *beast* within him is released. It is during the release of his internal *beast* that he may become very aggressive even feral with his Dominant which creates its own delicious variations to the *power exchange* dynamics.

The Switches Perspective:

Switches, those individuals both male and female, who straddle both sides of the Whip and embrace various aspects of dominance and submission at varying times tend to fall into one category more so than the other when with a specific individual. For example: being either dominant or submissive depends on the other person's nature. If their partner is also switch, they will alternate as desired even taking turns with who's the Dominant and who's the submissive.

The one benefit of being a switch is the ability to explore both sides of the spectrum—without guilt or shame—dominating another and submitting to them. However, if it's in your nature to be submissive (as with some sexual submissives), switching into Dominant mode may be short lived. Sometimes, these individuals are considered *"Service Tops"* or *"service bottoms"* depending on the service they offer.

Chapter 6

Those deliciously wicked things we do!

Now that we've discussed the fundamentals and the psychological aspects of Dominance and submission, let's put it all together to discover the emotional connections associated with all those deliciously wicked and sinfully erotic activities.

The essential thing to keep in mind when dealing with BDSM is to allow yourself to become what I like to call the *Sensual Scientist*. This is where you explore the mind—body connection for your characters. From the Dominant's perspective it's about allowing them to explore and derive sensual and sexual pleasure from what they do to their slave; thus exploring the physical and sexual aspects of control as well as pleasure and pain. From the submissive perspective, it's about being of service and letting go of their inhibitions and fears in order to be vulnerable to and with another, surrendering all they are.

Here's another way to look at the dynamics of a D/s relationship. Imagine for a moment that the dominant is a sail boat and the submissive is the sea; what amazing things they will experience together as they take their journey. The various storms along the way. The amazing silence that brings peace to the soul. Even all the creatures they'll discover along their path, both big and small—adventures both frightening and inspiring. Though it may not always be smooth sailing, it will be a new exploration of the core self each time as the individuals learn something new about themselves and each other.

There is no way I will be able to cover every possible effect of and every toy that is used in the scene, however I want to provide you with several scenarios and a little insight into how these implements feel on the body and the psychological effect they have on both the Dominant and the submissive.

Whenever possible, try these toys and/or activities on yourself before writing about them. One thing I know about writing erotica is that if you don't "feel" the excitement or fear or whatever emotion you're trying to convey, you won't be able to express it as accurately for your readers. Ensure to address all six senses—sight, sound, taste, touch, smell and the mental-psychic connection—to guide your novel during every interaction between your characters. This is the heart of the BDSM connection.

Before I forget, I want to address a little tidbit—if your characters are on a budget, many of the tools needed or implements they'd want to use can be easily purchased at a local hardware store or made from items purchased there. Home Depot or "Dom-Depot" as the community tends to call it, carries almost everything your characters need, including rope and of course wood so they can make their very own St. Andrews Cross to tie their slave up to.

As we discuss the various objects and implements used during *Scenes* or merely to enhance a couple's less formal interactions, it's crucial to remember that everything will feel different to the individual depending on their vulnerability and the comfort of their position as well as the exposure the activity provides. Thus what someone is willing to do in the privacy of their own home, they may not be willing to do in public. The reverse is also true as the more dangerous edgy interactions they may be willing to endure in public (with a Dungeon Master or others able to immediately come to their rescue) they may not engage in privately when there is no one to aide them. The vulnerability they experience in private with their Dominant as opposed to the exhibitionistic experience they had in public will also put a different emotional spin to the interactions.

Another thing to keep in mind is the feeling of vulnerability which the person experiences based on arm placement and their inability to move about. For example, having your arms tied behind your back will provide one sensation while having them tied over your head will bring another. It goes without saying that having a submissive's arms tied behind their back and then incorporating their feet (like being hog-tied) will increase the submissive's level of vulnerability. However, this position will interfere and limit which areas of the body will be available for the Dominant. For example, you wouldn't be able to use the slave's buttocks, yet his/her genitals would be exposed.

To give you a taste of what this feels like please play along with me for a moment and notice the different sensations you experience in each possibility I provide. Notice for yourself what feels comfortable, what feels threatening, what makes you sigh with boredom and what rives you up. Of course, your submissive doesn't have to be physically tied—the real surrender comes when the Dominant mentally bind the submissive, not needing ropes or restraints because the submissive knows that their surrender would please their Master/Mistress—thus in essence becoming the rope that binds them.

A little taste of wickedness:

For each example, hold the position for at least two to three minutes. Use an hourglass or loud egg timer to keep track of time. This will help you get the psychological feel as well as the physical. Become the *Sensual Scientist* as you take notice of your heart rate, your breathing, whether you quickly jumped from one activity to the next or whether you lingered in one more so then the other. Is there anticipation? Excitement? Nervousness? Embarrassment? Notice for yourself if you enjoyed the position or if your mind was busy thinking of different things you could "do to your characters" or "have done to them" in each position. This is just step one of all the various ways you can add to the mental and physical aspects of Dominance and submission and *Power Exchange* interactions in your books.

If you originally perform these exercises alone, try them with someone instructing you to do them. Note the difference and the vulnerability factor associated with each. If you really want to get a gold star in your *Sensual Scientist* role, explore the difference between a man providing instructions as opposed to a woman providing them. You will notice the dynamics will shift. Take note of which activities you bucked against and which you accepted easily.

Once you've taken instruction (been the submissive), take control—be the Dominant! Have a friend or lover perform these tasks for you. Exploring both sides of these exercises will help you develop your character as you analyze the internal connections they might feel.

If you can, use a full length mirror to enable you to see yourself in each position. It's not only the feelings and internal connections made which push the individual into *subspace* or *Domspace* its viewing themselves in that position even imagining what onlookers might see which pushes them over the edge. Remember that the mind drives the body. It is the seduction and capture of the mind that will tumble the person into the mindset of surrender or dominance; even the seduction and enticement to accept more pain. Whatever else you need to get you ready to explore—do it. Allow yourself to explore these positions it to the fullest.

Don't forget to add a little music to the background. You'll be amazed how the tempo and the words will affect your mindset. Even the emotional connections associated with the type of music you choose can change how you feel. Just as you create a romantic ambiance, create a D/s one. This is part of setting the scene. When performing your exercises, do the same, to provide yourself with the fullest possible effect.

Dare I mention the added sense of vulnerability you will feel should these exercises be done in the nude?

Exercise #1

Stand up and place your hands at the small of your back. Right palm over left. Fingers flat. Thumbs touching. Press your shoulders back and stand up straight and proud. Your eyes should be straight ahead. If someone is standing before you, you should not make eye contact. Correct yourself every time you do. If you're alone, place an object (like a statue) before you to represent a person; notice how often your eyes involuntarily drift to it.

Exercise #2

Place your hands behind your neck, pushing your elbows out so they are parallel to your shoulders. Stand with your feet shoulder width apart. Again use the eye contract restriction unless the other person instructs you to look at them. You may find that the eye contact restriction allows you to distance yourself a bit from the experience however making that eye contact could make you feel a bit giddy, nervous, shy, embarrassed, exhilarated, etc.

Exercise #3

Place your hands over your head, extending them upward as if they were tied to the ceiling, with your wrists together. Legs spread shoulder width apart. It'll amaze you to realize that if you spread your feet another two to three inches apart, the feeling of vulnerability will increase. And yet, notice that nothing new has been added. You're in the same position as before. Now close your eyes and let your head fall back. Don't forget to breathe. (Something a Dominant is often reminding a submissive to do. Funny how they forget to do that. It's a normal human habit to hold your breath when excited or in nervous anticipation.)

***

Remember to notice your reactions. Your breathing. Your body. Are your hands sweating? Are you cold? Notice your thoughts even though you are just doing these simple exercises to get a feel for what your characters might experience. Are you finding yourself trying to distance yourself emotionally from the sensations of vulnerability? Are you telling yourself, "This is silly" or are you becoming excited allowing your mind to wonder what could happen next? Have you slipped into the Dominant role and started to think about all those deliciously wicked things your characters can do to one another in each position?

93

Give yourself permission to experience everything. Later you can analyze it and rehash all the nuances and reflect on all those feelings you experienced.

Even not feeling "anything" is something!

***

Exercise #4

Kneel and place your hands in the positions mentioned above. Again, notice how each position creates its own emotional connection with nothing more significant than the placement of the hands, the eye contact or restriction, and even head placement. This emotional connection will change if a blindfold is incorporated especially if there are others in the room with you. Blindfolds are a wonderful tool to help a submissive focus on just the Dominant and/or just the experience the Dominant desires to share. The blindfold also increases their feeling of vulnerability.

Exercise #5

Get down on all fours. Hold yourself steady. After two to three minutes, let your shoulders drop to the floor while you push your buttocks upward, into the air. Each position creates its own sensation—its own sense of vulnerability.

Now lay on the floor on your belly and reach back to grab your ankles. Notice the feelings which arise—vulnerability—rebellion—each person is different. What parts of your body are exposed? Is it comfortable? Difficult to breathe? Lift your head up and maintain that position for two minutes. Can you?

***

I can keep going with various positions but you get the picture. As an author, exploring these positions for yourself will provide you with a realistic idea of what body parts and areas are exposed and vulnerable. Notice what's visible and what's exposed to the eye and/or an instrument/toy that might be used.

It goes without saying that performing these basic activities dressed would be vastly and erotically different than if performed in the nude with someone instructing you. Plus you'll also experience a different level of vulnerability, resistance, rebellion and so on depending on whether the person instructing/observing was male or female, friend or lover—or one of each.

Toys and Instruments for Delicious Torment

I want to address the instruments, Toys, and props used during *Play* and some of the various aspects associated with them; to give you a little flavor of what it would be like to experience and experiment with them.

You can view various versions of these items online. My two favorite websites/stores are Mr. S Leather www.mr-s-leather.com and Stormy Leather www.stormyleather.com.

Mr. S Leather caters toward the male and Leather Men community. They have the best quality leather and products on the market for both men and women. They also have extraordinary equipment to feast your wickedly creative mind upon. Indulge your wicked imagination about the various possibilities based on the equipment you find on their site or many others. It's like a Dominant candy store!

Stormy Leather caters more toward women, offering lots of great corsets. If you're looking for Plus Size women's apparel and ideas for clothing, Hips & Curves www.hipsandcurves.com caters to plus size women and carries a great selection of reasonably priced corsets and sexy lingerie. Feel free to research these websites to view the items I describe below.

Blindfolds

Good blindfolds have a fur lining which ensures the slave cannot peek by raising their heads and looking between the gaps inferior blindfolds leave just between their eyes and the bridge of the nose. Also, the fur will cushion the delicate skin of the eyelids creating a feeling of comfort which lures the slave into further surrender.

The beauty behind blindfolds is that it immediately intensifies anything you do. It is a Dominant's best friend. The submissive will immediately become hyper vigilant and aware of his/her surroundings. Their hearing becomes attuned to every small noise. Their heartbeat automatically accelerates. Their apprehension will increase as they try to decipher what the Dominant will do next. Plus if the Dominant moves away from the slave and stays quiet or merely observes, the slave often has an intense reaction— anything thing from feeling anxious, frustrated, fearful, tearful, etc. Some submissives/slaves may even feel a sense of abandonment if the Dominant remains quiet for too long and react with anger, even aggression, and demand to be set free.

The Dominant can let them struggle with these emotions testing them, allowing the slave/submissive to work through it themselves. However, it's never good to leave a submissive unattended. Just like with a candle, the slave/submissive can melt quickly or burn the house down. The Dominant can alleviate some of the submissive's fear by occasionally speaking or touching the slave softly then leaving them to their silence once more. Psychologically, this creates a major effect as most individuals aren't used to sitting in silence. Don't be surprised if the slave/submissive cries or becomes very emotional.

Imagine the shock the submissive will experience if they thought they were alone and they carried on a verbal conversation with themselves—out loud. Perhaps they displayed their anger or resentment at the Dominant for "leaving them alone". Would the Dominant punish them for it or chuckle at the behavior startling the slave?

When playing physically with Whips or another impact instrument, the blindfolds allow the submissive to feel the impact more intensely as they have nowhere to go but into their minds and their bodies. Using blindfolds pushes the slave into *subspace* more quickly especially during *Psychological Play* such as *Fear Play* and *Mind Fucks*. Therefore, if the Dominant character wants the slave to last longer and endure more, he shouldn't use the blindfold or should remove it after a while. Eye Contract restriction will work in lieu of the blindfold and you can reinforce the restriction by swatting the submissive if they don't obey.

Blindfolds are extremely effective when conducting *Mind Fucks* (Head Trips) as you want to create a sense of fear and time/place distortion. You can even introduce other players which may or may not touch the slave. However, the slave wouldn't know for sure who was doing the touching since he/she couldn't see. You could also have the Dominant disguise one hand in a Vampire Glove or a latex one creating other sensations. And if your characters were in a hotel room, the Dominant could order room service and torment the slave with the idea of being seen by the wait staff when dinner was delivered.

One couple I know was traveling in from different states and meeting up at a hotel in Chicago where the Dominant was hosting an event. As the slave was due to arrive first, they arranged that his Mistress would call him once her plane arrived and she was on her way to the hotel. The slave was instructed to be waiting in the room, kneeling in the corner, naked, his back to the door, with a blindfold on.

When the Dominant arrived at the hotel loaded with packages, the bell hop insisted on helping her take the packages into the room and bypassed her in his overzealous attempt at being helpful. As the bellhop entered the room and placed the packages down, he looked up to see the slave quietly kneeling in the far corner, naked, with his arms behind his back, and a blindfold over his eyes. It took the bellhop a moment to get over his shock before he quickly finished unloading the packages from the trolley and placing them in the room. The bellhop left with a huge tip and an interesting story to tell.

Though this was definitely not planned, the Dominant of course used the situation to her advantage, teasing the slave about being seen naked by a stranger. The Dominant then incorporated this embarrassing situation (for both of them, though she would never admit it to him) into actual *Play* and rewarded the slave for not breaking his protocol and maintaining the required position despite his shock at the bellhop's unplanned inclusion. She also incorporated a deliciously wicked *Mind Fuck* throughout their stay at the hotel as she'd tease him about exactly which bell hop had witnessed his surrender.

As you can see, blindfolds are a must-have!

Gags

Gags of any type are interesting little torture devices all their own. On the one hand, it makes a slave feel more vulnerable because no one will be able to hear him/her scream; yet on the other hand, it prevents the Master/Mistress from hearing her slave cry out or beg for mercy or respond coherently.

There are many different gags available, from the popular ball gag to the more erotic penis shaped gags. There are even gags with phallic shapes on the outside which the Dominant can then use for their own pleasure. There are dental gags that hold the mouth wide open to allow for oral penetration. The only bad part about these is they cause the slave to drool. Unless you enjoy that look, it's not the best gag choice. Of course, the Dominant would never dream of using their slave's unavoidable drooling against them, would they?

Because their ability to communicate with the Dominant is impaired, you want to provide the submissive with another form of communication. Placing a yo-yo in their hand, with the string tied around their finger to prevent it from rolling away or creating a possible tripping hazard is a good option. This will allow the slave to release the yo-yo if they are in distress and/or if they want to use their *Safeword* or for whatever other reason they might need to capture their Master's attention. Having the yo-yo tied to the finger prevents the Master/Mistress from having to search for it. The Master can then attend to the slave's needs, re-roll the yo-yo, place it once more in the slave's hand, and start anew. The yo-yo also acts as a warning device for poor circulation if the submissive forgets to bring such information to the Dominant's attention.

Restraints

There is a wide selection of restraints. Each will produce its own effect as well as a psychological connection. Rope has one affect. Metal another. Some individuals may feel comfortable with minimal rope restraints others will need total immobility.

You will find a different emotional connection with rope bondage as oppose to metal restraints. The only explanation I can think of is that metal restraints have a psychological perspective of being permanent and unbreakable, plus it has the additional factor of added weight on the submissives wrists and/or ankles; and on the body if you encased them in chains. And perhaps with ropes, there's an unconscious belief that you can bite through them or cut through them somehow if necessary where you can't do that with metal handcuffs. There's also the punitive aspect of handcuffs and the feeling of being "caught" just like a criminal. Rope does not have the same punitive association.

There are various restraints which are specifically built to take comfort into consideration. Many of the leather cuffs used for restraints are fur lined. This aides the submissive in remaining in them longer. The really good quality Suspension cuffs are build with a piece of metal that the submissive can grab onto while being suspended giving the slave the illusion of control and serving to help take weight off the wrists.

Some submissives are only interested in bondage and do not need any further interaction as the feeling of vulnerability from having their bodies immobilized is erotic enough to them and they neither want nor need any further stimulation. For these individuals, it is the Bondage itself which sends them into *subspace*—a submissive's feeling of euphoric release.

Rope Bondage

There are various levels of Rope Bondage and degrees of expertise. Look up Midori or Steve Speliotis and you'll discover some beautiful depictions of Rope Bondage. The most important aspect of Rope Bondage that needs to be addressed is its intimacy. When you are tying someone in intricate knots and positions, you are spending hours with them—literally. This is one of the reasons submissives love to be tied up in rope. They literally have their Master/Mistress' complete attention and focused on them. Some experienced Bondage players can maneuver the body into intricate designs while still keeping the submissive comfortable.

Rope Bondage creates its own level of intimacy and *Play*. I once watched a woman place a man into Rope Bondage from start to finish. I was fascinated by the interchange between this Mistress/slave couple as well as the intricacy of what she was doing. The end result was that she'd created a *human chandelier* complete with little tea lights/votives strategically placed along his arms and legs and hanging crystals which she place in various areas to hang from the rope. However, it was the connection between them which was so sensual and romantic at once. Her soft words of encouragement while she artistically arranged the rope around him. The expression of trust and affection on his face as he looked up at her or nuzzled his cheek against her shoulder as he sought to connect with her or her palm every now and then wanting to feel closer to her was breath taking to watch.

Predicament Bondage is another form of *Rope Play*. This is where the Master/Mistress ties the slave in such a way that moving one area of their body will create movement and discomfort in another area of their body creating a live marionette. For instance, tying the right hand across the body so that it is resting against the slaves left breast with the rope continuing down the back and tied to her right leg, which is raised up off the floor. Her right arm is further tied to a harness rope that she has around her waist so that when her right arm moves to allow her right leg to touch the floor the arm will pull on the harness and the rope threaded through her legs will rub against the sensitive areas of her genitalia.

Another Predicament Bondage scenario could have her harness rope connected to her neck collar giving her just enough maneuverability to bend over in an uncomfortable position. If she were to straighten up, this would tug the harness against her genitals.

You can also perform Predicament Bondage with nipple clamps. For example, securing one end of the clover clamps to a male's nipple then securing the other end to his scrotum (or a woman's labia) will create an interesting situation. The slave would have to bend over slightly for this since the chain that connects the clover clamps (nipple clamps) is only so long. As he's being Flogged or Whipped, he will instinctively jerk his body even straighten up depending on the severity of the impact of the Flogger or Whip. This reaction will cause the clamps to tighten on his ultra sensitive body parts where the clamps were placed.

For men who are uncircumcised, you can have the clamps on their foreskin. Oh those delicious cries of pain they'll create! The Sadist will love it. You want to ensure to gather enough foreskin so as not to accidently tear the foreskin. Remember the whole point of Predicament bondage is to annoy and to set up a situation where the submissive creates their own discomfort and torment by moving.

As Rope Bondage can take hours, some Masters/Mistress' avoid using rope and opt for the quick leather cuffs or metal restraints since for them, the fun begins once the submissive is tied up. Then again, some Dominants don't want to be that intimate with the submissive/slave and leather or metal cuffs work great. This isn't to say that these types of bondage aren't intimate but that Rope Bondage creates a "different" sense of connection between the Dominant and the submissive.

The beauty of Rope Bondage doesn't end until sometime after the ropes are removed. The rope itself leaves behind marks and indentations on the body once removed that will last for a few minutes or few hours depending on how long the rope was tied to the body. These rope groves form its own erotic sensation for both the Dominant and the submissive.

At times some discoloration may occur especially if the rope was used to bind the penis, breasts or other body parts in awkward positions. Personally, I don't find skin discoloration erotic thus I avoid it. Plus there's also the safety factor of blood circulation to consider. When in doubt, play it safe is my motto.

For men, discoloration can also occur if he's been placed in genital bondage and he becomes erect as his girth presses against the ropes creating a pleasure/pain effect causing the blood to pool into the tip of his penis, thus discoloring it. Not to worry, this discoloration will go away. If you maintain the arousal, the slave won't know whether to choose to be released from his bonds or beg the Dominant to let him climax within them—yet another form of dominance and surrender. A great book for CBT (Cock and Ball Torture) is *Family Jewels* by Hardy Haberman. Hardy provides wonderful ideas on ways to torment a man in his most prized possession.

With Rope bondage, as with any other bondage or restrains, the Dominant must always ensure the slave has proper circulation. This can be assured my pressing your pinky beneath the ropes or beneath the restraint. If you can press your pinky comfortably beneath the restraints, you typically have enough leeway to prevent poor circulation. If not, the ropes need to be loosened to avoid permanent nerve damage. Another way to check for good circulation is touching the skin and fingers and feeling the coolness of the skin. Too cool and there may be circulation restriction.

You can also have the slave squeeze your hand while you notice if there's enough pressure when they do. If they're not in *subspace* they should be able to squeeze normally, if they can't this may be an indication of a circulation problem. These are basic tricks used by Dominants when checking circulation. I'm not a medical doctor, I am a Clinical Sexologist and my rule is always, when in doubt, release the rope and re-wrap it.

Of course conversing with the submissive is imperative to ensure the rope isn't over joints or isn't creating excessive discomfort. If discoloration begins, releasing the rope or repositioning the slave may be in order.

Before you begin any bondage session, you always want to take into consideration any physical and/or medical ailments the submissive may have such as diabetes or circulatory problems that may affect their submission. This is definitely one of those times SSC/RACK is in effect.

As for the use of ties, scarves and nylon stockings in lieu of actual rope, this isn't recommended as these items actually tend to restrict blood flow and become quickly entangled knots. That beautiful $50 plus scarf or tie you love will most likely be ruined or have to be cut off after a night of play. One trick to getting a knot out which most people don't realize is that if you roll the knot between your fingers or palms, it will actually loosen the knot and allow you to unravel the knot easier. Remember patience is needed when playing with rope.

One item you always want to have handy when using rope is *rope scissors*. These are merely a few dollars therefore you can purchase a few (have your character purchase a few). Keep one in the toy bag, one in the dungeon, one in the car, etc.

Hoods

Hoods are a wonderful form of control and psychological play! Depending on the type of hood you purchase, you can control what the submissive/slave sees and hears thus playing with sensory deprivation and taking the scene to a higher level of intensity. I've found that hoods allow the Master/Mistress to be more detached and sadistic with their slave than they would normally be as they are not confronted with the "face" of their submissive and thus can objectify him/her more easily.

For Dominants who enjoy the aggressive nature of their slaves, they can designate the times the slave wears a hood as a *free pass* to allow their aggressive nature out to play without fear of repercussions. Then again being tormented because he/she was *naughty* is a reward in itself sometimes.

Of course, like the blindfolds, if the hood is used for sensory deprivation, it will affect the interactions of the slave as well as the Master/Mistress more quickly.

Nipple Clamps

One area that most authors get wrong in their BDSM descriptions is the sensations it produces is the nipple clamps. Yes, nipple clamps hurt going on because they pinch and prolonged or severe pressure will create cracking of the skin; however it is when the clamps are removed that the real pain begins and the severity of the pain is in direct proportion to the length of time the clamps were left one. Thus a clamp left on the nipple for 5 or 10 minutes feels great when it's removed; however, one removed after 30 minutes produces major pain. As with other areas of the body needing circulation, you do not wish to go longer than 30 minutes not only because of the level of pain it will produce but the possibility of nerve damage.

Imagine what it's like when your foot falls asleep and those needle prick sensations rush up your leg. Now multiple that by 20, 30 even 50 percent. That rush of re-circulation is what creates the pain and will bring tears and screams from the submissive. To minimize the pain, press your thumb or palm against the nipple to regulate and slow down the returning blood flow. Experienced submissives will actually beg you *not* to remove the nipple clamps after they've been left on for a while because they know the agony of pain awaiting them.

Clover clamps are actually the best clamps to use as they tightened when you pull on them thus keeping a good grip wherever you placed them. Nipple clamps can also be used in other areas of the body such as the genitals, the male's scrotum, the underside of the arms etc. There are larger and tighter clamps available for use with the scrotum. Purchasing the clamps which incorporate a chain is actually best as you can tug on the chain in order to torment the submissive further.

A great way to incorporate a *Mind Fuck* and have the slave torture themselves is to have them hold onto the chain attached to the clamps. Place the chain in their mouth thus keeping it out of the way while Flogging them. As they jerk their head, they'll pull the chain. Since the chain is only so long, lifting their head would automatically tug on the chain. And of course if they drop the chain then that must mean they desire the Dominant to tug on it, doesn't it? Don't forget, it's the psychological effect that triggers *subspace*.

Nipple clamps can also be used on the tongue; however the basic wooden clothespins work best for this purpose as they're bulkier and more uncomfortable. There really isn't a fear of the tongue swelling and causing breathing restrictions as long as only the front tip is pinched. Be warned, this activity will lead to drooling. Yet, the Dominant can always punish the slave for drooling even if he/she cannot avoid it. Besides, don't all naughty slaves deserve a good tongue lashing—or was that leashing?

Another tidbit of the lifestyle an author needs to know is since men's nipples are smaller and thinner than women's, it's harder to keep them clamped. The clover clamps do a great job at securing them as the clover clamps collapse onto itself tightening when pulled. The psychological effect on a man as focus is given to this part of his body, which is ultra sensitive and often overlooked is astonishing.

Clothespins will also work well as they have a larger surface and can grip more. Using clothespins around the scrotum or on the penis itself (especially for uncircumcised men) is beyond erotic. If you purchase the colored clothespins you have a more decorative look as well. Care should be taken with the plastic clothespins as these have a tighter grip as opposed to the wooden ones. Also, the smaller plastic clothespins can tear the skin if used in *Zippers* or ripped off the body while using a *Flogger* or *Whip.* Some Dominants will sandpaper the wooden clothespins to ensure a smooth surface to avoid splinters—especially given the delicate areas these clothespins will be placed in.

Vampire Gloves

These are gloves made of leather or soft fabric which have little spikes embedded in the material facing outward. The spikes are thin and less than a sixteenth of an inch long. Think a third of the size of a thumb tack but not as sharp. The Master/Mistress will run their gloved hand over the slave's body and occasionally press down or squeeze different body parts such as breasts, penis, or even *Spank* the submissive's buttocks. This creates a wickedly sinful sensation.

Chastity belts

The ability to control the orgasm of a slave is a powerful aphrodisiac and highlights the *Power Exchange* especially for men as they are used to being sexual whenever they desire. Placing a slave in chastity leaves no doubt in their mind that their body is now the *property of* their Master/Mistress.

There are several types of chastity belts on the market for both men and women. Some are very simple and others are extremely elaborate. The entire purpose of the chastity belt is control.

Some chastity devices are specifically designed for the penis or vulva. Others incorporate both the genitals and the anus. Most devices are secured with an external lock. Some of the more elaborate chastity belts have an internal locking mechanism as opposed to an external one. There are several devices for men on the market made from a clear plastic material. Personally, I like metal cages myself. There is just something very medieval about them. Some male cages have bars while others have the area completely encased in metal.

There are some chastity devices that incorporate plugs which are inserted into both the anus and vagina which are locked into place adding the additional component of discomfort and arousal. As these are more invasive, the psychological aspect of control is more pronounced. Still other devices have vibrating dildos for their insertable pieces.

For men, there are chastity belts designed like cages which make it difficult for him to become erect and if he does, the bent or restricted position in which the penis is kept will increase the discomfort and pain he experiences. The fact that the Dominant controls the slave's ability to remove the device and end the discomfort further establishes the control and creates a pleasure/pain dynamic which reinforces the Dominant's control and creates a synergistic effect.

Most Chastity devices have a built in hole in them that allows the individual to relieve themselves without having to remove the device. The hole is enough to allow for urination but not penetration. If no urination hole is provided, the individual would have to ask for permission to relieve themselves—thus surrendering their control more profoundly to their Master/Mistress.

A metal device adds the essence of actual weight on the slave's hips constantly reminding them of its presence. Though there are several devices for men that are clear plastic, cheaper and lighter to wear, they don't have the psychological impact of a metal device—something some Masters/Mistresses enjoy adding into the mix. Some devices are designed for prolonged use and individuals may be placed in them for a few hours to a few days or weeks. This extended duration reinforces the psychological component as well as the *Power Exchange*.

There are also lightweight plastic penal chastity belts as well which can be quite handy for a slave who is traveling and wants to avoid metal detectors at the airport or who has metal detectors at work. Although be mindful of new TSA screening protocols. (I have to chuckle at this possibility.)

Don't forget that uncircumcised men left in prolonged chastity will have to clean daily beneath their foreskin. There are special swabs on the market for this. Daily cleaning can also become a ritualized event with their Dominant's presence or assistance; even if it is over the phone.

Chastity devices can cost anywhere from $75 to $2,000 or more depending on the design and their intricacy. Some are specially customized for the individual man or woman and are tailored to their body specifications.

Anal sex

Anal sex is one of those activities which most men and women consider taboo. Because of this, it is one of the areas and sexual activities that become most profound in a BDSM relationship regardless of the gender dynamics.

Anal sex is also one of the activities most authors get wrong when describing penetration and sexual pleasure. Here's a quick anatomy lesson. The anus is actually shaped as an S-curve and has two curves. Penetration that is done hard and fast and "straight in" will cause extreme pain and discomfort as the penis or the strap-on will slam into the back wall of the anus. This incorrect penetration can actually lead to damage and rupture of the rectum and anal wall leading to serious complications and in extreme cases death. A slow penetration is required. After penetration is achieved, a stronger harder thrust can be employed.

Another tidbit most individuals overlook is the fact that the anus does not produce its own lubrication thus the need to use artificial lubrication is essential to avoid micro-tears in the anus as well as minimize pain. Though if the purpose of the penetration is to cause discomfort, to exert dominance, then no lubrication will effectively cause the pain desired.

Here's another must know! Anything inserted into the anus that doesn't have a large round base or a handle/string to hold onto it or keep it outside the body will be absorbed and sucked into the rectum necessitating a trip to the emergency room. The same is true for items such as alcohol or drugs introduced into the anus as they are immediately absorbed into the bloodstream due to the thin lining of the anal walls.

Anal sex isn't just about penetration! There are many erotic and fun activities you can do including teasing, anal rimming, finger and tongue penetration and of course the highly advance and dangerous sexual activity of *fisting.*

I'd recommend that any author who's writing about anal sex especially those writing about male-male romance read a few books on the topic of anal sex to learn the basics. Two of my favorite books on this topic are *Anal Pleasure and Health* by Jack Morin and *The Ultimate Guide to Anal Sex for Women* by Tristan Taormino.

Impact Play

Impact play can be performed with a variety of instruments. These instruments or toys as they're called, can include Floggers, Whips, canes, paddles, etc. basically anything that is striking the body. To avoid actual injury to the submissive/slave, regardless of the instrument used, avoid striking joints and/or putting pressure on them. The kidney area as well as the eyes, face, and head should be avoided. Care should be taken when striking the soles of the feet as all the body's meridians (nerve endings) terminate there. Anything else is fair game!

It is best to strike on fleshy areas of the body as the impact will be absorbed more readily. Skinny submissives tend to bruise easier and have less of a "cushion" to their skin during impact play. It is also easier to draw blood from *Impact Play* with skinny submissives.

If you are slapping the face, the Dominant should place one hand against the opposite check before striking. This will help minimize the Whiplash effect on the neck and impact to the face preventing damage to the neck or eyes. Yes, eye damage can actually occur from severe face slapping as the Retina may become detached from impact.

When using Whips, you want to avoid cracking a Whip near the head area as the Whip is actually moving at speeds that break the sound barrier and it can damage the ear drum.

Though Whips are great fun to use, they do take lots of practice. Many Masters/Mistresses have struck themselves with a Whip now and again when they've caught a ricochet. Often the Dominant will have their free hand up to guide against the Whip wrapping around them as it comes back when they're sliding it from side to side over the slave's body.

Bull Whips aren't typically used (expect for show) as they will cut skin. Single *Tail Whips* are the norm. They provide a sting to the skin and though they will produce welts, cut the flesh and make the slave bleed; it takes much more force and repeated strikes for them to do so.

Candle/Wax Play:
The trick to candle wax is the height from which you allow it to drip on the body. The closer to the body the wax is, the hotter it will be when it lands on the skin. The best candles to use are those 99 cent prayer candles you can purchase at most food stores. These candles are bigger and last longer allowing for hours of fun. Another plus to these candles is the tall glass jars they come in makes it easier for you to hold it without burning yourself and allows the wax to melt sufficiently to drip it slowly over the submissives back, breasts, genitals or anywhere you desire.

Light a few jars at a time to have plenty of melted wax at your disposal to drip over your slave. If you purchase various colors you can also create art on their body.

Some Dominants enjoy melting a lot of wax, using a designated slow-cooker crook pot and brushing the wax over the submissive's body then using a Knife to carve symbols or words into it. The warmth of the wax will create its own unique sensations.

I once had a male Dominant convince me to allow him to brush the wax on my back. He swore it was the most orgasmic experience I'd ever have. Though I'm not submissive, I agreed to allow him to do so to see what it was like. Within five minutes of him starting to pour the wax over my back and brushing it on thick, I fell asleep. To me, it felt like being covered in warm clothing and so peaceful I promptly fell asleep. I opened my eyes once when he tried to "scare me" by telling me he'd use his Knife to scrap the Wax off my back. Since I trusted him, I merely fell back asleep. He did not appreciate my response. My "failure" to respond as he expected—as his submissives had in the past—frustrated him.

He insisted that if he poured the wax over my breasts I would experience the orgasmic sensation he was talking about. To appease him and my own curiosity, I allowed him to pour the wax over my breasts. Other than a slight heated sensation when he purposely dripped the wax closer to my skin, I again fell asleep thinking of being covered in warm blankets and clothes just coming out of the dryer.

I share this with you to stress the importance of mindset and the psychological connection for the person receiving this or any other activity. To me it was warm and comforting, to others—submissives—it was erotic and orgasmic. To that Dominant male interacting with me, it was frustrating as I didn't respond the way he expected and desired me to. Thus, here's another possibility to keep in mind when writing about your character's reactions—mindset! Remember, an individual with a Dominant personality will never response with the same emotional connections as a submissive or a slave.

As candle wax is messy, you may wish to purchase a single bed sheet that you can discard afterward. Washing it would ruin anything that's in the wash with it and leave bits of wax behind to ruin other loads. To minimize ruining your bed or kitchen table, use an inexpensive shower curtain liner or plastic sheeting. (Again check Dom Depot it's only a few dollars!) Place the liner underneath the bed sheet you plan to toss away or use the shower curtain liner by itself to catch all the drips and protect your bed, table, or carpet/floor.

For a person who's hairy, the Wax will cling to their body hair making it painful when removed. A trick to prevent the wax from clinging to the body hair is to use baby oil. Massage the baby oil over the body before dripping on the wax. Never use baby oil prior to *Fire Play*! This will actually burn the skin and can cause problems as it will allow the fire to burn longer then desired on the body.

If you want to be erotically creative, have your Dominant character use a knife or straight razor to help remove the wax from the body—even shave the submissive's genitals at the same time. Or you can use a thin comb and comb through the wax matted hair on the chest or genitals for an added sadistic twist.

Another creative way to remove the wax from the body is to use a Rubber Flogger. However this will only work well if you dripped the wax on the body not brushed it on. This type of removal is messy as the flecks of the wax will fly everywhere. This is better done outdoors or in a public Dungeon otherwise you'll be vacuuming bits of wax from the floor and furniture for weeks.

Fire Play:

Fire Play is an advance skill and considered a form of *Edge Play*. Yes, it is very dangerous. It is definitely something an individual should learn to do with a Mentor. It is performed in two different ways. One is by using a gauze stick dipped in alcohol and coating different areas of the body with it than igniting the alcohol. The other way is by using the gauze covered metal sticks which are soaked in alcohol already lit (on fire) than running them over the body.

The trick to *Fire Play* is in the timing! You don't want to leave the fire on the body more than a few seconds. One hand sets the fire, the other whips it down and away. There is an erotic beauty in the way Fire ignites on the body and how the blue flames rise making the submissive arch and cry out as it heats their body. The Dominant isn't attempting to harm the submissive thus great care is taken to prep the area and the submissive/slave to avoid accidents and injury.

As I mentioned earlier, never use baby oil or creams and lotions on the body before engaging in *Fire Play* this will make the fire burn longer and can cause burns and blistering. It should go without saying that you want to avoid the face and hair areas.

There are a few technique/tricks that you can do which are fun and add to the eroticism of the act. One is where the Dominant brushes the alcohol on their palm, then ignites it and then places the *Flamed palm* upon the submissive's flesh. Another is what I like to call *Fire Spankings*. This is where you spank the slave using the burning Fire sticks.

Some individuals prefer their submissive/slave immobilized—others allow the slave/submissive the freedom to not be restrained as accidents can happen and if the submissive needs to move or "drop and roll" because of a spill or something, not being restraint allows them to do so. However, it also leaves the submissive/slave free to get up and run if they panic which can cause its own risks.

Ensuring that the alcohol does not drip into any "creases" or body cavities where you can't immediately extinguish it is essential. Remember, the Dominant doesn't want to burn the submissive, merely provide them with a heightened sense of controlled fear. Another thing to consider is the fumes from the alcohol and flames which will get to you after awhile. Ventilation is a must! However, you don't want to have a fan blowing or the windows opened because if there's suddenly a major breeze it might take the fire places you'd prefer it didn't or blow out the flames before you're ready. Air conditioned rooms are best.

Some submissives will quickly enter *subspace* because of the combination of fear, pain, and physical sensations they experience in their body created by this major endorphin rush. The Dominant will want to watch for enlarged pupils and slow responses or incoherent ones—all signs of *subspace*. Remember, a submissive will want to endure for their Master/Mistress so they'll push themselves to take more even when their body isn't able to. It's the Dominant's responsibility to safeguard their slave and taper their own desires accordingly.

Hairy slaves should shave a few days before they engage in *Fire Play*. The smell of burning hair is a turn-off and definitely not erotic during a *Scene*. Combining *Wax play* and *Fire Play* may be interesting especially if you're using the Wax to remove the hair. However, the skin will be extra sensitive to *Fire Play* and the slave may not be able to endure as much.

For *Fire Play* you'll want to always have a fire extinguisher handy as well as a wet dish towel. The wet towel will serve as a way to cool down the body and if any accidents occurred or the fire was left on the skin to long and blisters develop, this will help. Have a can of sunburn Spray handy as well. Spray this over the body after play as it has a little bit of antiseptic and analgesic which will help numb the skin and allow it to heal.

As I mentioned above, this is one of those activities you should be trained in before performing it on your own. I do not recommend this activity for the beginner.

Fire Play is all about the sensual connection and the eroticism. Care should be taken not to get drawn into the beauty of the flames.

Mummification

Mummification is a fun way to play and immobilize a submissive. The slave should be naked or wear minimal clothing as their body temperature will rise significantly—imagine being in a sauna. As the submissive/slave will have trouble standing and keeping their balance, you want to ensure there is a chair close by or somewhere soft they can lay back on or fall into.

If your characters are playing around water, be extra careful that the slave is able to breathe and remain in the shallow end of the pool as he/she will be completely vulnerable and helpless—even floating will be difficult for them.

Mummification can be performed with a few rolls of *cling wrap* and duct tape. Start out with the *cling wrap* putting it loosely over the body areas you want. For example: around the shoulder and down to the wrist, trapping the arms against the sides of the body. You don't want to make it tight as the plastic will automatically tighten as you circle the slave with the wrap. You can have the slave turn, however I prefer the Dominant either circle the slave since you don't want him/her to get dizzy. You can also just reach around them and layer the *cling wrap* around the body.

Here's another important tidbit to add to your *Scene*—place a few cotton balls over the nipples when you start encasing the slave. The cotton balls create a buffer between their skin and the *cling wrap*. This will allow you to safely cut into that area once you're done wrapping them to expose their nipples so you can torment them as you please.

Once the *cling wrap* is in place, you can now layer on duct tape which immobilizes them further. Again you don't want to put it on tight. The *cling wrap* will tighten on itself and the duct tape on top of it will make it even tighter. You don't want the slave so uncomfortable there's a circulation problem or their breathing is restricted; this would require you to cut them out of it immediately. Also, you don't want to put duct tape directly on the skin as it's difficult to remove and may tear the skin—especially in delicate areas. It goes without saying that you don't want to put duct tape directly on the hair or the face. Personally, I'd caution against placing it on the throat area as you don't want to restrict respiration especially if you also have the chest bound.

If you want to wrap the head with duct tape, use a hood where the face is exposed or at the very least the nose and mouth are exposed completely. Again, the Dominant must watch respiration and any restrictions to the same very carefully. (If the slave has Asthma, ensure you have the inhaler handy.)

You can use arm length pieces of duct tape to fortify the hold in specific area as you desire. Using various colors of duct tape and *cling wrap* will allow your characters to be more playful. However the clear wrap will allow the Dominant to keep track of body color. Typically it will take approximately 20 to 40 minutes to completely mummify your submissive.

Once the slave is wrapped, the Dominant can play as he or she desires with their very own *live mummy*!

Engaging in sexual activities while the submissive is thusly bond is erotic and psychologically enticing as you would literally make the submissive nothing but a sex object exposing only his/her genitals, anus and breasts area.

When you're ready to end the *Scene*, simply use a pair of scissors or a knife to cut the slave out of his/her bondage. With mummification, you want to slowly expose the skin to the air. It's essential to remember that the slave's body temperature will have risen significantly and exposing it to quickly can cause them to faint. As they're tied, you want to ensure they don't tip over since they won't be able to break their fall. It's best to start releasing them by cutting away from the bottom, allowing the slave further access to their legs so they can sit down or lay down before you release them completely.

Be aware of *subspace* which will affect their coordination and coherence. Another safety issue to keep in mind is that they will become dehydrated while wrapped, therefore, ensure to have plenty of liquids (water) available for them to drink while mummified especially if they're in it for an hour or more.

Never combine fire with mummification!

If you're doing any kind of *Breath Play* or *Waterboarding* (an advance form of drowning), keep the slave at the shallow end of the pool. This is paramount to ensure their safety.

I do not recommend *Waterboarding!* This is an extremely dangerous activity especially without an assistant or when performed with a newbie who will most likely panic from the overload of emotional and psychological fears.

Mind Fucks:
One of the most astonishingly sadistic tools in the Dominant's arsenal is the *Mind Fuck* or Head Trips as some

call them. The beauty of the *Mind Fuck* is the fact that by being evasive or creating a distortion in perception, a "double think" scenario were two truths co-exist simultaneously, if you will, you confuse the mind and push the submissive over the edge without the need of any other instruments. The book, *The Forked Tongue* by Flagg has wonderful examples of how to create some exceptional *Mind Fucks.*

It's easier to give you a few examples of a *Mind Fuck* than to try and explain how to create them. Therefore, below I've provided a few simple examples of how they have been used in previous *Scenes.*

The submissive was bound and blindfolded as he felt the knife against his flesh. At the last minute the Dominant turned her hand dragging the sharp edge of the knife handle against the submissive's stomach. The submissive cried out thinking he'd been gutted. This misconception was further reinforced when the Dominant stuck her fingers into a glass of water then ran them over the submissive's flesh in the same area she'd dragged the handle of the knife using a wiping away motion and saying, "Damn, you're bleeding."

In another *Mind Fuck,* the submissive had been used hard and had some genital torture performed. When he'd put his underwear back on the Dominant noticed that the submissive had dripped some ejaculate on the fabric but said nothing about it. A little while later the submissive stated, "My underwear feels wet" wherein the Dominant promptly replied, "Oh, I didn't think I cut you that bad".

Though in each case there had been no real damage, the thought and the emotional connection lead the submissive to feel fear and further psychological torment. Some submissives thrive on these types of psychological and fear-based interactions; others cannot tolerate them and break under the pressure which places *Mind Fucks* at the top of the list of advance *Edge Play.* Because of the psychological upheaval experienced, though it may be sadistically scrumptious for the Master/Mistress it can be very emotionally draining on the submissive. You may find that the slave reaches *subspace* much faster than normal during a *Mind Fuck.*

The bad part about a *Mind Fuck* is that it's mentally and emotionally draining on the submissive causing them to hid *subspace* quickly and once there unavailable to *Play* further. Also, if the submissive panics or an old fear/psychological wound is triggered, the Dominant will have to walk them through it and/or end the interactions or redirect their *Scene*. Then again, perhaps the purpose was to create "panic" and fear and help the slave overcome it and learn to desensitize that fear. The *Mind Fuck* has so many possibilities!

The major caution I can provide is to be careful with the issues and scenarios you pick to *Play* with when engaged in *Mind Fucks* as some themes can open up a door to emotional pain and the need for professional psychiatric treatment; and of course, a loving Dominant would never want that. You want to *Play* rough with your toys but not break them!

***

It's essential to remember that much of what's done in BDSM affects the individuals not only physically but even more so psychologically regardless of whether they're coming at it from a Dominant or submissive perspective. This psychological connection is why BDSM relationships are inherently much more intense and develop more quickly than vanilla connections even without physical/sexual interactions. The need to belong, to serve another, to interact and feel powerful or connected is the driving force behind every Master/slave relationship. When writing your romances, reinforcing this connection and addressing how it is not merely physical but at times an indefinable psychological and spiritual connection will help your readers better understand the D/s dynamics you are building.

A note of caution! Several of the ideas and interactions I've provided in this book and in this chapter in particular are considered *Edge Play* and are extremely dangerous to engage in. Please remember when using them in your novel that someone may try to mimic what you write. Throwing in a line about the Dominant having educated him/herself prior to introducing this technique with their slave would be a good idea. Though I believe in RACK principles (Risk Aware Consensual Kink), I would object to any *Edge Play* and even some basic *Play* being performed without the Dominant, at the very least, educating themselves and learning a little about how to keep the slave safe.

BDSM is about a loving caring interaction with another human being not a cavalier way of getting off on an erotic scene; thus, ensuring the physical, mental health and wellbeing of both the Dominant and the submissive should always be the foundation of any interactions.

Chapter 7

Training a Slave
Protocols, Rituals
&
Corrective Measures

The natural progression of training a slave/submissive is that when he/she enters into the relationship he/she is trained in the *Protocols* and *Rituals* of their Master/Mistress. Once these protocols and rituals are provided, the submissive is required to adhere by them. If the slave does not, he/she is corrected, punished and finally dismissed if all else failed to correct the situation and elicit the desired behavior. Let's break this down a little further for you to follow the concepts of each phase in training a slave.

Protocols & Rituals
As with any other relationship there are established rules and guidelines which need to be adhered to. The major difference between a *vanilla* relationship and a BDSM one is that these guidelines which govern how an individual is to behave while in the relationship, what is acceptable, and what will not be tolerated, are hashed out and negotiated at the beginning and reinforced, expanded upon and changed as time goes on. Whereas, in a *vanilla* relationship it's assumed that each individual knows how to behave and knows what is expected of them so that when they go against what their partner expected fights ensue or the excuse of "I didn't know" is used.

These guidelines and requirements that are established prior to commencement of the relationship are achieved by way of *Protocols* and *Rituals* and enforced by corrective action, punishment if necessary, and finally dismissal if all corrective measures failed to rectify the situation.

Protocols are a set of guidelines established by the Master/Mistress for the submissive/slave to follow to help them know what is required and how they are expected to behave and perform. These *Protocols* may be elaborate or simple. The purpose of the *Protocol* is to reinforce the submissive/slave's position in the Master/Mistress' life every time they perform the act. It also gives the submissive/slave a sense of belonging and accomplishment they may not otherwise have in their vanilla life. In case you're wondering, the submissive can also request a specific *Protocol* or create a *Ritual* which makes them feel comfortable or safe and share this with their Master/Mistress having it incorporated into their actions when serving.

Below are a few examples of kneeling *Protocols* for a slave to conduct when in the presence of his Master/Mistress:

Kneeling straight up to show respect with his hands at the small of his back and his eyes straight ahead or downcast is the common form of presentation and shows respect. The slave may be allowed to rest on his heels with his palms on his thighs awaiting the next command from his Master/Mistress.

Another position can find the slave kneeling supine, his body resting on the floor, arms outstretched as if bowing before a Queen and awaiting her next command.

Some submissive/slaves are allowed to stand instead of kneel especially if in Dungeons or at an outdoor event, or if the slave has knee problems. Under these circumstances, the submissive/slave may be required to stand in accordance with the prescribed *Protocol*. This may be to stand at attention or Parade Rest as they do in the military while in the Dominant's presence. (Parade Rest is where the submissive stands with their arms behind their back, their legs shoulder width apart, their head held high looking straight ahead.) You may consider this the slave's "ready position" as he quietly waits to be of service—standing silently in the background until he is called for.

Some Dominants institute eye contact restrictions *Protocols*. This is where the slave is required to never look the Dominant in the eyes. This *Protocol* reinforces the hierarchical mindset of BDSM. A submissive/slave would then be corrected or punished if he/she fails to adhere to it.

Some *Protocols* require a slave wear a certain type of uniform or wear nothing at all while serving. One Master/slave couple I know instituted a dress code where the slave wears a plain white blouse with a long dark colored frock dress over it along with flat heeled shoes—a very conservative attire. The Master also wears a type of Victorian suit that's very professional looking and in keeping with his business responsibilities. If you met this couple you would never think they were kinky. They look like your average wholesome ma and pa neighbors.

Don't forget what I said before about BDSM lifestylers being the people you see every day sitting next to you on the bus or at church or at work—or perhaps in the mirror.

The list of possible *Protocols* is endless and each Master/Mistress can tailor the *Protocol* to what they require of their submissive/slave adding their own flair as desired.

On top of *Protocols* are *Rituals. Rituals* are established either separate from or in conjunction with particular *Protocols.* For example one *Ritual* may be that when the submissive/slave returns home from work, he or she is required to bath, consciously and metaphorically washing away their *vanilla* persona then kneeling naked in a designated area.. During this time of quiet reflection, the slave reorients him/her self to the life they have chosen with their Master/Mistress and also release their outside worries and stressors. Once the designated time has passed or the slave feels they're ready, he/she would rise and go about their duties in the household and/or present themselves to their Master/Mistress as per the established *Protocols.*

Another *Ritual* can govern the way the slave/submissive offers themselves for use prior to engaging in BDSM activities with their Master/Mistress whether in private or in public.

Below is an example of a *Ritual* a Dominant woman created for *Her* slave which is used when they engage in public *Play*.

The *Ritual* begins with the slave preparing the area for them to use. The slave lays out a red lap blanket on the floor where she's designated they will conduct their *Scene*. This serves to establish a boundary for onlookers not to cross. The slave then sets out the *Toys* from her *BDSM Toy bag*. Once that's accomplished, he places a chair for her to sit on directly across from where he'll kneel to allow her to observe him for as long as she desires. By preparing the area, he shuts out everything from his mind. Once the *Scene* is ready, he undresses completely and kneels on the blanket, closes his eyes centering himself and focusing on being of service to his Mistress in any manner *she* desires of him. The slave may be embarrassed and feel vulnerable to be so exposed before others as he awaits his Master's dictates yet he does so anyway as he knows it brings *her* pleasure to have him so exposed.

As the Dominant sits in the chair, she is able to observe her slave's diligence and attention to detail. In a way, she too is preparing herself for the *Scene* to come.

The *Ritual* continues when she joins him on the blanket. She strokes his hair and reassures him of her presence. Before she binds him, she raises his face so he may look into her eyes, brushes his lips with hers, nibbles his lower lip and tells him how pleased she was by his efforts. She then kisses his wrists before she places each wrist in the leather cuffs which she then connects to the ceiling beam overhead.

This is a sweet sensual *Ritual* for this couple. Not all rituals have to be sensual, some are pragmatic others are forceful. Everyone's *Protocols* and *Rituals* vary and are unique to them. You can put any twist you desire to them. The only thing the Dominant has to keep in mind is that He or She is responsible for reinforcing these *Protocols* and *Rituals*. If the Dominant isn't willing to put the effort into upholding them, they shouldn't be established as it'll create bad habits in the slave/submissive and make the submissive/slave wonder at the level of dominance they are actually receiving.

As I mentioned before, the submissive will often test their Master/Mistress and purposely mix up the *Protocols* or *Rituals* or perhaps not adhere to them to see if their "naughty" behavior will be corrected. This test isn't done out of childishness, disrespect, nor malicious intent but in an ffort to reassure themselves that their Master/Mistress values them enough to care that they're doing a good job in following the established rules of the household and that the Dominant is willing to punish them when they're not.

Some slaves/submissives may demand a higher level of control requiring their Dominants to impose "absolute measures and punishments". These slaves may leave a relationship if their more extreme needs are not met. Without these strict controls, the slave doesn't feel "right" about the relationship. There is nothing wrong with this. As we've discussed, every individual has their own needs and should find the best relationship for them—just as is done in the *vanilla* realm.

Before I move on to corrective measures, I want to talk a little about training a slave to accept pain and become orgasmic from it. Though the training is much like anything you wish the submissive/slave to learn, when training a slave to accept pain, you must slowly introduce it and connect it to their sexual release. You also make pain a reward they receive for being good such as receiving a *Spanking* or a Flogging. The difference here is that you're constantly increasing the level of pain or emotional intensity associated with what would otherwise be a punishment. This emotional connection is what will eventually have the slave/submissive needing even begging his Master/Mistress for more since he will have associated his pain with the pleasure of fulfilling his Master/Mistress' needs. In this way, you seduce the slave with his/her need for pain; and thus have also begun his pain training.

As for how you would punish a slave you are training to except pain, you would withhold their ability to interact with you and share your time and essence.

<u>Pain Training</u>
A submissive/slave can be trained to enjoy pain even learn to orgasm from it. The trick is to seduce them into it! This seduction is accomplished by using their own desires to achieve the Dominant's objective. For instance, the slave wants to please his Mistress/Master, therefore he/she will try to accept what the Master/Mistress desires and finds erotic.

The truth is that as the body starts experiencing pain and the adrenaline and endorphins as well as DHEA are released into the body, it can register the stimulus as either pleasure or pain. It is the individual who places a psychological and cultural significance to the stimulus deeming it good or bad, pleasure or pain, which the mind and body will then accept accordingly. This is no different than the old belief of "no pain no gain" that athletes thrive on; or the military Rangers who use the fact that when they "feel pain" it's a reminder that they're still "alive".

In order to help the slave embrace the desire for pain or to be able to tolerate it better, the Dominant must link sexual and/or emotional gratification to it thus having one sensation override the other and conditioning the slave to desire pain as a way to achieve pleasure. Employing Pavlov's salivating dog experiments (classical conditioning) and the principles behind behavior modification will help achieve this connection. I find that having the slave count through the pain allows him/her to be seduced into the idea that the pain will go way as soon as they reach a certain number. The counting also provides a sense of accomplishment and the slave feels pride in him/her self that they were able to endure the pain for the duration of the count. This sense of pride is especially true for masochistic individuals as it services to reinforce the pleasure/pain connection.

Of course, this feeling of accomplishment deserves a reward. The reward can be a kiss on the boo-boo or a sexual treat or another reward previously agreed upon of a sexual or affectionate nature. It can be anything the Dominant chooses to bestow on his/her slave for being so brave and enduring for them.

Corrective Measures

The natural progression of a slave/submissive when entering into a relationship is that he/she is trained, corrected, punished and finally dismissed if all else fails. Here's how it works.

The submissive/slave is trained to do a specific task. If the submissive does not understand or does not follow through on what is requested or required, the submissive is corrected. If the correction provided does not remedy the situation, punishment is administered. If training, correction, or punishment doesn't correct the behavior dismissal from service will result.

Below is an example of the natural progression to training a slave/submissive on performing a specific task.

The submissive is instructed that when he is told to present himself for inspection, he will stand with his arms behind his back, right palm over left, fingers flat not interlocked, shoulders pressed back, head held high, eyes straight, feet slightly apart. (This is the same position as Parade Rest in the military.)

The submissive follows all the instructions; however, he erroneously placed the left palm over the right. His Master/Mistress will then correct the position talking him through it once more. If he again errs he is again corrected and made to perform the presentation several times until the Dominant is sure he has it correct. Tomorrow or a few days from now when he again is instructed to assume this position and fails to do so properly, the Dominant has several forms of corrective measures to use, whether that is to retrain the individual to reinforce the proper way to present himself or to use punishment.

Let's break down the corrective measures further so that you may see what it looks like and how it leads to behavior modification. If you want to know how to institute change and the value of "punishment", review a few therapeutic manuals on behavior modification as well as a few books on Dominant guidelines. For our purposes, we're going to get the "down and dirty basics" to help the Dominant elicit the behavior she/he desires from their submissive/slave.

It's imperative to remember that when dealing within the *Power Exchange* there's only three choices when it comes to corrective measures. Understanding which comes first is essential in establishing the foundation of the relationship and ensuring it flourishes to its utmost potential. As with any other relationship, if you address the issues before they become problems and communicate effectively you can create a joyous union. If not, you'll create a nightmare you'll long to escape from which will only serve to make you feel inadequate and frustrated. Nowhere is the old adage *you reap what you sow* more true than when in a BDSM relationship.

Corrective measures are not about making the person feel bad nor humiliating the slave and should follow the pattern of training, correction, punishment and dismissal. Punishment should never be your Dominant character's first choice. Like with your story plot, you want to build up to Punishment not "jump to the deep end".

Here's how it works: if the slave does something the Master/Mistress doesn't like, then *training* is the order of the day. It's the Dominant's responsibility to mold the individual into the slave/submissive they desire.

Imagine it like starting a new job. Your boss or supervisor (the Dominant) will teach you what is required and how it's done in that job (*Protocols*). If you mess up and your supervisor doesn't correct you or didn't provide enough training then it's really not the new employee's fault—but the supervisor's.

Now, if the employee (submissive/slave) is provided with the adequate training (*Protocols*) necessary and is still not meeting the expectations, then *correction* is necessary. At this point, the supervisor (Dominant) will go over what is required and even have the employee (submissive/slave) recite the requirements to him/her to ensure the employee is correct and if necessary reword or clarify any confusion there may be.

As we continue with this example: if despite the *training* the employee (submissive/slave) was provided he is still unable to follow through appropriately and still makes mistakes or his performance is not acceptable, then it's time for the Master/Mistress (employer) to consider the following:

(a) Is further training appropriate?

(b) Does the *Ritual* or *Protocol* need to be changed?

(c) Should the slave/submissive (*employee*) be referred out for *specialized training*?

(d) Is *Punishment* the correct next step or is *Dismissal* warranted?

In a work situation, corrective measures could mean loss of pay or commission even suspension. Specialized training can be made by assigning the employee (submissive) to another boss or trainer (Dominant) or sending them to a specialized training course (slave training academy as outlined in the Resources chapter).

In a BDSM relationship, *corrective measures* could be physical such as a Spanking, Flogging, even humiliation or sending the submissive for training to another individual or organizations (such as a Slave's Retreat like Catherine Gross and other individuals and various BDSM organizations provide). Again, this is no different than in the *vanilla* realm where the employee would be sent to Human Resources for training or sent to an outside agency for management development.

If after a predetermined time the situation doesn't resolve itself, *Dismissal* (firing) should be considered. *Dismissal* is where a slave/submissive is advised that they will no longer interact with the Dominant and ties are severed. The submissive/slave will also have their collar removed.

Losing their collar is a traumatic incident for a submissive/slave as this means they no longer *belong* to their Master/Mistress and any interactions in the future will be limited or non-existent. This is as devastating as any break-up in a *vanilla* relationship is, if not more so, because of the unique dynamics of the D/s relationship. Depending on the length of time the Master/slave were together it can even be as traumatizing as a divorce.

Yes, I am purposely making the connections between the *vanilla* realm and the BDSM realm as it's important to realize that the two are intertwined and have the same emotional connections. People don't stop being emotional human beings merely because they enter into a BDSM relationship. These relationships aren't merely a compartmentalized part of someone's life, it is—in many instances—their core identity and who they are despite not sharing it openly with everyone in their lives. Thus when entering into a BDSM relationship that isn't just for *Play* or a one-night stand/one-kink stand, the emotional connections are strong.

The responsibility for lack of training and the dissolution of the relationship falls primarily on the Dominant's shoulders. It is the Dominant's fault for not guiding the submissive/slave where they needed to go; unless of course guidance was provided and the submissive choose not to follow it or constantly fought against it. At that point, dismissal is the most appropriate course of action.

As with any other relationship, if one party is constantly fighting or not giving their all than that is not a relationship you want your characters to stay in. And though women are often "people fixers" always wanting to help improve the person they care for or love and make them "better"; in a Dominance and submission relationship, this can be very detrimental to the Dominant's mental health.

You can't force submission! It's either freely given or it wasn't there to begin with. Besides, trying to force submission is like trying to force someone to love you—it'll never happen.

Often you'll read in a romance or hear in real life that the *individual* presented a "challenge" and they were taught to be a great submissive or slave. This does occur. However, there is a tremendous difference between someone being a "challenge" and someone fighting the Dominant for their submission every step of the way. One you enjoy, the other you're tearing your hair out. And though everyone loves a challenge, no one enjoys *Mission Impossible* or beating their head against a brick wall repeatedly.

The closest way I know to describe this dynamic is this: imagine you like a man and you want to date him. He plays a little hard to get (a challenge) and you pursue him harder. This is good. Now imagine he's gay. This is what it's like to fight someone for their submission. Mission impossible!

As for what types of punishment your Dominant characters would administer to a submissive/slave, this would depend on the offense and the nature of the Dominant. Every Dominant has their own manner of *Punishment*, their own hard limits. For instances, a Master/Mistress who's service oriented may provide the slave with a hated task or use humiliation to *Punish* them. A Sadist or typical Dominant may use pain as *Punishment*—a Flogging or Caning, etc.

Though a slave being inappropriate and disrespectful once or twice can be corrected through the use of *Punishment*, if this is a constant thing, then he/she is not someone your Dominant character would want to be in a relationship with as it'll be an uphill battle—again, the difference between a challenge and mission impossible. Realistically speaking, who wants to be in a relationship where their significant other disrespects them constantly? Staying in such a relationship shows lack of self-esteem on the part of the Dominant and a need to work on their own issues which in essence provides you with possible plot development and food for thought.

The same can be said of a Dominant who is constantly disrespectful to a submissive. Unless this constant disrespect is purposefully part of the dynamics of the relationship because both the submissive and Dominant get turned-on by it, (remember we previously discussed how some people enjoy being humiliated), then this Dominant is actually pushing the bounds on the relationship and in some instances being abusive within it.

I previously mentioned the fact that many submissive women look for a Dominant man in the *vanilla* realm only to find an abusive one instead. The same can be true for a submissive man. We cannot overlook the fact that some Dominants and submissives (men and women) may enter into the BDSM community with ulterior motives disguising their malicious nature behind bratty behavior or a sadistic façade. Oftenmembers of the community can spot these individuals quickly and word gets around about them. In the end, the BDSM community is like any other, you have your good and bad.

The ultimate *Punishment* would be *Dismissal*. Once *Dismissed,* the Master/Mistress may decide not to interact with the slave further in any manner. The slave/submissive's collar will be removed and any financial connections will severed. If the slave was a member of the Dominant's household, he/she would be required to vacate the premises—much like what happens during the dissolution of a marriage.

So now that we've addressed the basic steps to incorporate into any slave training program (Training, Correction, Punishment, and Dismissal), let's dabble into the heart of punishments and humiliation as a corrective measure and as actual *Play*.

Chapter 8

Punishment & Humiliation Play

It may not surprise you to discover that *Humiliation Play* can also be used as *Punishment*. However, you may be astonished at the emotional connection these two types of interactions have on the individual—both Dominant and submissive.

In this chapter I will provide you with various examples of Humiliation Play which can be used as Punishment, or to help motivate the slave/submissive, or to provide an emotional or sexual release. You'll also discover how *Humiliation Play* can be used as an aphrodisiac and how some individuals actually thrive on it.

As the connection between these two intensely emotional areas of Dominance and submission are at times indistinguishable, I want to start with *Punishment* and lead into *Humiliation Play*. Whereas Punishment is mostly for punitive reasons, like Humiliation it can be used for either punitive or erotic reasons as well. Let's start however with punishment from a punitive perspective.

Punishment

As I previously mentioned, the severity of the punishment should be indirect proportion to the offense committed. For example: the first time a slave/submissive is perceived to be rude his Master/Mistress can address the behavior with a verbal reprimand—thus following the progression of *Corrective Measures* we previously discussed. If this is the slave's second or third offense, he/she can receive a *Spanking*. Punishment can also be administered if the slave did not follow through with a task or did not complete his task in the time allotted.

Punishment can take the form of a Spanking, sending the slave to the corner for a "time out" (yes, like a disobedient child), or giving the slave an hour of practice getting into the position with which he struggles. The choice of corrective action and punishment is at the sole discretion of the Master/Mistress. Punishment can even be sending the submissive home and not engaging further with him/her that day thus depriving the slave of the time they wished to share with the Dominant based on their own actions. And though yes, this temporary dismissal will also deprive the Dominant from sharing time with their submissive, the Master/Mistress never wants to reward bad behavior, otherwise they end up with a brat and no one enjoys a child throwing a tantrum even less so when the "tantrum" is being thrown by an adult slave/submissive.

A good guideline for the Dominant to follow is never to use a submissive/slave in pleasure on the same day he/she is punished!

Another important factor about correction and punishment is that it shows the submissive/slave that their Master/Mistress considers them valuable enough to correct their behavior. This correction and punishment helps strengthen the emotional bond between the two. It creates a measure of calm and peace within the slave as he/she realizes that someone will be there to call them on any inappropriate or dangerous behavior making them feel appreciated and loved.

It is not uncommon for a submissive to at times purposely instigate punishment—most often he/she will do so on an unconscious level; however some slaves do so purposely and again this behavior should not be encouraged as it undermines the *Power Exchange* and is in fact very disrespectful on the part of the slave.

However should the Master/Mistress notice or feel that the submissive is purposely failing to complete the task, and this is a consistent pattern of passive-aggressive behavior, the Dominant may choose to *dismiss* the submissive altogether and discontinue this toxic relationship.

Keep in mind that *Punishment* doesn't always have to be physical in nature. Some punishments can be psychological in nature as well which at times can be more effective. Here's an example of a psychological punishment: Tying a submissive up and then refusing to touch them, just leaving them tied for a period of time in an uncomfortable position. Don't forget to add the hourglass or egg timer to keep track of time. For an added twist, let them know beforehand that they'll have to remain in that position for two turns of the hourglass or two rings of the bell. Thus, they'll regret the fact that they thought they were almost done as the first turn of the hourglass was done only to remember they had one more to go.

Even worse yet is tying your slave up then using another submissive in front of them showing your slave what he/she missed out on because they were bad—because of their own inappropriateness.

It's important to remember that just as Masters/Mistresses are territorial with their submissives and their property, slaves/submissives can be as well. They know a good Dominant is hard to find and will therefore not want to share them or risk losing their Master/Mistress to another submissive. Thus this punishment in particular is very effective. Plus, the Dominant can teach the slave that just because they must punish the slave by not allowing the slave to play, the Dominant doesn't need to suffer the same fate.

Male Dominants are more likely to engage in sexual activities with the other submissive more so than female Dominants are. This I believe is a cultural norm regardless of whether in the BDSM or vanilla lifestyles. For their part, female Dominants can cuckold their male slaves forcing them to watch their interactions with another man. It's imperative to keep in mind that because of the *Power Exchange* dynamics, a Master/Mistress can openly choose to engage in sexual activities with others yet deny their submissive/slave the same liberties.

However playing with another slave regardless of gender can be a double-edged sword as some submissives will require sexual monogamy from their Master/Mistress. Of course, once the Dominant gives their word on sexual monogamy, it cannot be broken (not even justifiably broken) as it would destroy the trust the slave has in his/her Master/Mistress and the entire D/s relationship. Betrayal can go both ways and without trust BDSM relationships are too dangerous.

Keep in mind there are many ways to be sexual within the BDSM community without actually having intercourse with another. Thus the couple's definition of sexual interactions will come into question. Therefore, if sexual monogamy was the agreed upon boundary in the relationship for both individuals, this does not prevent the Master/Mistress from using another slave to Whip, Spank, Flog or tease in some other way. Gotta love those loop holes!

Punishing the submissive with something they hate or hate to do is also very effective. For example, if they hate to scrub toilets, making them scrub the toilet with their toothbrush is very effective punishment. If they hate peeling potatoes, buy 50 or even 100 pounds of potatoes and have the slave peel each one. Then have the slave cook every dish possible with those potatoes—mashed potatoes, potato salad, French fries, potato pancakes, potato soup, etc. The Dominant can then give the food away to friends or have them over to enjoy it while the submissive is sent to his room or sent home and the meal is enjoyed without the slave's presence; thus, the slave isn't able to receive any praise for the food or feel good that the food was appreciated. Not only would the punishment be provided, it would also be reinforced by the slave's absence from the festivities as he is not yet deserving of their Master/Mistress' time.

Okay, I'm sure you're getting the picture here. I can continue with many more examples however I believe you'll come up with some wonderfully devious ideas of your own.

Many of the examples I've provided in the *Humiliation Play* below can also be used as a form of *Punishment* as well. If you want to be really creative you can emulate those old Hollywood Chinese Kung Fu Masters. For example: make the slave kneel on uncooked rice with a bucket of water in each hand. Or tie them down and Spank them until their buttocks were black and blue. Some Dominants use a bamboo cane or similar instruments to punish until they draw blood.

Below are a few additional behaviors associated with reasons for *Punishment* that you'll want to address and/or avoid with your characters. These examples will also give you some ideas on character development and help you create more believable BDSM characters and romance novels. As I've been doing throughout this book, I am writing to you as the writer and to your characters as the Dominant and submissive.

For the sake of simplicity and to avoid confusion, it's easier for me to address these issues as if I'm advising another Dominant. Thus bear with me as I present the information to you as if it were for personal use for yourself—after all, in a way you are your characters.

A Dominant always wants to be careful of a slave/submissive who does things for the sake of *Punishment*. This is evidence of an individual who's either a S.A.M. (smart-assed masochist—major brat who lacks respect), or a player (someone who's there only to get off and will be a waste of your time).

A Mistress/Master who's not comfortable with administering *Punishment* or doesn't enjoy it may want to pass a more masochistic slave/sub on to a friend and find one that's more to the Master/Mistress' temperament. It is not uncommon for some Masters/Mistresses to not participate in physical BDSM activities and desire solely service-oriented activities from a slave/submissive. However, if you want to keep this particular slave (the masochist), a great option would be to designate a friend or fellow Master/Mistress as the "Punisher". This would allow the masochistic slave to experience the "punishment" he/she needs as you sit regally before him watching him be Whipped by another at your command.

It's imperative not to "baby" the slave/sub during *Punishment* but to reinforce the fact that "it's regrettable that **his/her** actions lead to this". If you want to throw in a little more into the *Punishment*, you can have the slave hooded/blindfolded so he never sees the person that performed the *Punishment* or have the person dispensing the *Punishment* hooded adding to the *Mind-Fuck* principle. Everyone is afraid of the hooded man—he has no mercy!

Another way to *Punish* him could be by denying him the ability to interact with you and playing with another as you force him to watch—even if you have to tie him up and leave him hanging there while the Master/Mistress takes their pleasure with another—whether physically or sexually.

Another reason to *Punish* a slave is if you notice the individual is leaving every decision up to the Master/Mistress. This can be a sign of complete surrender which is wonderful, however, it can also be a sign of someone who wants to take *no responsibility* for their actions and these slaves/submissives will become a source of frustration to the Master/Mistress. Though it's great to have a slave who surrenders completely, it's boring to have one that gives you no input and thus doesn't give you the feedback you need to push against to challenge you to be a better Dominant and/or give you that thrill of having really pushed your slave/sub into another level of physical/sexual surrender.

If the Dominant recognizes that his/her slaves are constantly getting into trouble or that negative behavior pattern are common in the relationship, these problems may be caused by the Dominant and not the submissive. One factor which can cause this is the Dominant not having appropriate or clearly established *Protocols* or *Rituals* for the submissive/slave to follow. In this case, the Dominant needs to do some internal work on themselves and perhaps undergo some training of his/her own.

A final reminder about punishment: never reward a slave on the same day you *Punish* them!

The slave has to be reminded that their behavior was inappropriate and will not be tolerated.

Humiliation Play

Let's take a look at Humiliation Play. One of the primary focuses of *Humiliation Play* is behavior modification as well as a catalyst to improvement and increased self-esteem. It may surprise you to discover that for some men and women it is a tremendous turn-on and aphrodisiac. On another note, Humiliation also services as a wonderfully creative source of *Punishment*.

Men more so than women seem to thrive on humiliation, even connecting it with sexual desire to a level beyond the typical "talk dirty to me" phrases. Though there may be a psychological basis for this erotic connection, the actual possibilities vary and if you're interested, you can research it further. The simplest conclusion I can provided is the one provided to me by a submissive woman I know. She stated that as a woman she was used to being put down and humiliated in many different ways by various people throughout her life: the teachers who didn't think she was as smart as the boys and thus overlooked her efforts; men who catcalled as she walked down the street or thought they could paw her as she danced with them at a club, even lovers and family members who were inappropriate. Therefore, she did not want it as part of her D/s interactions. She went on to theorize that as men were used to being at the top of the food chain and didn't experience the humiliation women did nor at the same level, they could more easily eroticize it.

Humiliation takes into account several different areas of a person's psyche and can vary in degrees of severity and purpose. To elaborate, Humiliation Play can include: embarrassment, degradation, self-esteem issues, self-worth issues and more. It can be performed in private or public. It can be overt or subtle. It can be for behavior modification, correction of inappropriate behavior, for sexual stimulation; and yes, even for encouragement and motivation.

I can already see you shaking your head telling me no one would use humiliation for motivation; yet haven't you goaded yourself into doing such things in the past. Haven't you once argued with yourself saying, "You're such a chicken if you don't..." merely to motivate yourself into taking that necessary but fearful step forward? Haven't you ever heard guys talking with each other, saying, "Man up dammit? Or my favorite, "You throw like a girl!" when they want the boy to do better.

The simple truth is that humiliation is used by everyone to some degree. Parents use it with their children to get them to clean their room or behave; sprinkling the humiliation with a bit of guilt and shame as well. The parents aren't trying to be particularly hurtful or malicious they're just trying to motivate and/or correct behavior. Here are a few examples:

137

Look at your room—do you live in a pig sty?
What will your friends say if they knew you wet the bed?
Stop crying. Take it like a man. Do you want them to
think you're a baby?

Some teachers use humiliation in front of the whole classroom to push their students to do better or to curb unwanted behavior. I remember having to put gum on the tip of my nose in school and walk to the lunchroom with it struck there because I dared to chew gum in class during grade school. And what about the kids that couldn't read well but were forced to read out loud?

Before we judge these behaviors, let's not forget that the military uses humiliation to reinforce and create the soldiers it desires taking humiliation to an art form that not only modifies behavior but establishes a new foundation and, ironically, builds self-esteem along with it. Spend some time with a Drill Sergeant or a traditional martial arts instructor and you'll be an expert in no time by merely observing their technique. Unlike the old Drill Sergeants who yelled and screamed at you, it's the quiet Drill Sergeant's like the one in the movie "Biloxi Blues" with Matthew Broderick that you should fear the most. That's the true Sadist, the Master/Mistress who controls you by having you control yourself through fear and apprehension, even anticipation, of what He or She would do next. And like the military, your parents and your teachers, the Dominant uses *Humiliation* to create the slave/submissive they desire.

When looking at humiliation from a sexual perspective it is important to remember that we all have our limits and our triggers. For example: calling someone a "whore" in public out of the blue may be embarrassing and undesired and lead to a confrontation. However, calling your slave "your whore" or telling them you "want to see how dirty your whore can be" allows them to overcome their inhibitions and embrace their *slutty adventurous* essence. It's amazing how having the slave call him/herself *your whore* opens that door. I dare say it'll give you a thrill as well.

With men, I find that using their fear of their penis size inadequacies will attain one of two responses: either it'll make them more assertive and aggressive, wanting to prove to you what else they have to offer; or it'll make them meek and submissive opening the door for you to attain further service from them as they desire to make up for their short comings in other ways. Even using their sexual experience against them of their explored or unexplored desires of same sex interactions will foster control for the Dominant.

Though you may see some of these examples, as well as some of the ones below as degrading or immoral, consider for a moment that it is a *Power Exchange* between two individuals who do so with a conscious desire to be open to each other in such ways. One being vulnerable and the other the aggressor—the catalyst for whatever emotional or sexual needs the activity fulfills for the two parties—and most important of all, it's consensual!

Again, I'll remind you that this behavior is not pathological in any way. It is merely a form of *Power Exchange* and perhaps sexual gratification as well as emotional release and healing that can be experienced in a D/s relationship. Sometimes, working through a *Humiliation Scene* allows the individual a way of releasing the pent up negative emotions they stored in their psyche, in their body, which needed to be purged. In this case, the Dominant is working as a pseudo-therapist to help the individual work through the issue creating the break in the slave's armor that's needed.

It goes without saying that an intense *Humiliation Scene* requires tremendous *Aftercare* which an ethical Dominant would ensure to provide whether through themselves or another. Also, it's often overlooked that not only is the submissive affected by an intensely emotional *Scene* but the Dominant is as well—typically more so when the Master/Mistress had to push someone they cared about or loved to such an extreme and hear them beg and plea for them to stop or be pushed further still in order for them to achieve the release necessary. Remember "no" and "stop" are not *Safewords;* therefore the slave allowed the *Humiliation* or *Punishment* to continue.

Unfortunately, I cannot tell you how to know when this "emotional release" is reached. It is different in every slave and it is something most experienced or *natural*

Masters/Mistresses sense *internally*. It is like having faith in a way as it's something you can't describe or quantify, you just *know*. It's an instinctive knowledge that can't be delineated yet can be learned with experience and dedication to the craft. It is knowing how far you can take a person before breaking them!

For those Dominants who don't have this natural instinct, whether because of lack of experience or because they're not in tuned with the submissive, they can learn this point by watching the signs and body language of the submissive and of course if he/she calls out their *Safeword* letting you know they've hit their limit. However, most ethical Dominants will halt interactions before the submissive reaches critical mass—before they break. You should torture your toys but never break them. No one wants to break their slave! Good ones are too valuable and rare.

So what's it look like? What examples can I provide that will help you when writing your BDSM romance? It goes without saying that you can use any of these examples for your novel whether BDSM or *vanilla*—and/or experiment with them in your own relationships.

Below I have provided a few examples of *Humiliation* techniques and practices which can be used regardless of gender as well as a few more specific examples which are gender based. Feel free to modify these examples as you wish for your characters. Yes, you can incorporate and integrate physical and sexual components within your *Humiliation Scene* to reinforce ownership and/or push the slave further as you deem appropriate and/or as you desire. However, unlike with *Punishment Scenes* and interactions where a reward would be inappropriate as you are purposely "hurting" the submissive due to their own misbehavior; with *Humiliation Play,* you can reward them afterward with sex or physical stimulation—or merely loving care.

The trick to *Humiliation Play* is in your creativity and using it to *Mind Fuck* the submissive/slave. Plus, again, *Humiliation Play* can also be used as a form of punishment. The true essence of *Humiliation Play* and why it works so well at curbing behavior is pride. It is the ego—the slave's pride—that you want to push against. Tapping into their pride and ego will provide you with the results you desire to make the slave feel, whether it's for behavior modification, punishment, sexual abandonment, or merely torment. Don't forget, as I mentioned before, some submissives both male and female actually thrive on humiliation. It's that extra push they need to overcome whatever obstacles prevent them from embracing certain aspects of themselves fully. And let's not forget it can also be a sexual turn-on.

Examples of *Humiliation Play* scenarios for either gender

Writing:

Making a submissive write 100 times, in pencil, "*I will obey my Master,*" or "*Naughty boys/girls are punished and don't get to play,*" will actually work wonders at curbing unwanted behavior. Not only does it reinforce your control, it makes them have to consciously tell themselves whatever you have them write out. Requiring them to write it more than 100 times will actually loss the desired effect. You want to use what they already know, what's been ingrained into their psyche. We've all had this type of punishment used against us when we were little by parents or teachers. Having them use a pencil instead of a pen is also a psychological factor which works in your favor as it'll piss them off to be treated like a child. And let's face it, we all hated to feel like a baby. Also, having the submissive perform such a *childish* task is humiliating in itself as they're reminded for the length of its completion that their behavior was inappropriate and childish. I can almost guarantee they won't do whatever they did again. And if they do, then a higher level of humiliation/punishment should be instated.

The Dominant should make it a point to count each line written to ensure the quote or line given was actually written 100 times. It's not uncommon for a submissive to use this punishment/humiliation (or any other) to "test" the Dominant's resolve.

The submissive will always test the Dominant seeing how much they can get away with and how *strict* the

Dominant will be with them. These tests by the submissive/slave will create the underlying foundation of the D/s relationship thus the Dominant never wants to neglect His/Her duty in this regard.

Corner Time

As children we all hated to be sent to the corner for a *time-out*. Again, you're playing on the individual's pride and ego by treating them like a baby who can't behave properly and is sent to the corner to stare at the wall for however long you, the Dominant, designates. To show that you're treating them as an adult whose actions are those of a child you can have them kneel in the corner on uncooked rise with their hands behind their neck or at their lower back. You can even set a cooking timer to have it beep when their punishment is over. A timer that ticks off the seconds, like an Egg timer— or better yet, an hourglass—adding a psychological component to the *Humiliation* as it constantly reminds them of their misdeeds. We discussed this factor in the punishment section as well.

Another way to use corner time is to make a small circle on the wall about the size of a baseball using chalk. Now place a penny or small coin against the wall and have the slave/submissive lean forward and hold the coin against the wall with their nose. For submissives who can't kneel for long periods of time, you can have them perform this *Punishment* standing up or sitting in a chair and leaning forward. The point is they must hold that coin against the wall the entire time using only their nose. If the coin drops for whatever reason, their time starts again. A good length of time is thirty minutes to one hour. Beyond that time, the psychological factor of the punishment can be lost.

Of course you can help motivate them to ensure they don't drop the coin again by having them pull their pants and underwear down and lay across your knees for a quick *Spanking* before they're returned to their task of holding the coin against the wall.

The Dominant should never interrupt a punishment or humiliation task that's given even if the submissive cries or tries to talk you out of it, or begs to be let off or forgiven because they're sorry. The Dominant should not allow bad behavior to go unpunished nor cut the punishment short. The Dominant can acknowledges the submissive's sincere regret then continue with corrective measures.

The Dominant wants to ensure to stop the timer or turn the Hourglass on its side for the duration of the encouragement as you don't want time to run out while you're providing encouragement. Believe it or not this reinforces the commitment of the submissive to improve their behavior. Subconsciously, the submissive will remember that the Dominant/Master will hold true to what they say; something essential for the submissive to believe and trust especially when they're interacting on other levels such as *Edge Play* or other physical interactions. Once the encouragement is over, the Dominant would begin the timer or reposition the hourglass and allow the task to be completed.

Using an hourglass or a noisy ticking timer is actually a great psychological enhancer to not only *Humiliation Play* but *Punishment*s and *Mind Fucks* as well. The ticking itself reinforces the agony of the duration of the punishment constantly reminding the slave there's still a lot of time remaining until the punishment is over; making 30 minutes seem like an eternity.

Much of what's done in BDSM affects an individual psychologically whether from a Dominant or submissive perspective, reinforcing behaviors and/or connections should always take this into consideration. This intense emotional connection is why BDSM relationships develop so much quicker and become more emotionally encompassing within a short period of time as opposed to *vanilla* connections.

Sleeping arrangements

Sleeping arrangements are a major source of *Humiliation Play*. They can also be used to either punish or reward. A Dominant can have their submissive sleep at the foot of the bed or on the floor instead of in the bed beside them because of a transgression or as a way to reinforce that only a cherished submissive would be allowed to sleep with his Master/Mistress. Having the submissive/slave sleep at the foot of the bed or on the floor also reinforces the control and mastery of the Dominant. The difference between a *vanilla* woman demanding her husband sleep on the couch, kicking him out of his own bed, is that act is about anger and this is about dominance and the *Power Exchange.* Remember it's all in how we look at it and what we call it that separates the vanilla world from the BDSM one.

Another subtle from of *Humiliation* and *Power Exchange* is having the slave wear nothing to bed while the Dominant wears a nightgown or pajama bottoms. This reinforces the power dynamics. If the submissive is shy, this requirement will push at their boundaries helping them open up more and become more confident and sexually accepting.

For some women being naked will really push at their boundaries as women aren't used to being naked anywhere but the bathroom or if they're alone in their own room and never for bed. A daring woman might sleep without underwear but rarely without a tee-shirt or nightgown. For males who are used to being naked for bed, you can use the reverse and require them to wear pajama bottoms or a chastity belt to bed so they'll remember their penis is the *property of* their Master/Mistress and it's exposed only at their command.

There are so many more examples I can provide however I'm sure you are getting the gist of it. Remember *Humiliation* can be used to tease the slave, elicit behavior modification even encourage the slave to grow. So many things can be viewed as humiliating or embarrassing, it all depends on the emphasize placed on it and what you incorporate with it.

Warning: never use humiliation on any behavior you enjoy and want the slave to keep. You can tease them about their behavior however if you use humiliation the slave may curb that behavior or erase it altogether from his/her repertoire.

Light Humiliation – Teasing— embarrassing moments

Before we get onto higher levels of *Humiliation Play*, it's important to realize that lower levels can elicit great rewards for both the slave and the Master/Mistress as it'll encourage and allow the slave to sit outside their comfort zone and do so in a safe manner knowing they're accept and cherished. It is using "teasing" and "embarrassing comments/actions" that only the Dominant and submissive know about. For example: the Dominant whispering in the submissive's ear something sexual which makes them blush in front of others or reminding them how *slutty* they were just hours before. Even running your hand over the slave's rear briefly can be a little embarrassing and yet be totally acceptable in a *vanilla* setting.

Personally, I enjoy teasing a slave in public by word or deed in ways no one is the wiser. It allows him to feel wanted and pushes his boundaries a little bit further encouraging him to be "naughty". It also allows me to be naughty myself as I share something with him that no one else knows about. Our secret!

Let me give you an example of what this looks like:

A few years ago, a friend took her slave with her on a book signing tour. She had him wear a collar around his neck that said WHORE in big silver letters. He wore it underneath his turtle neck sweater so no one saw or knew he wore it. Every now and then when he'd come to the booth to check on her or ask if she needed anything, soda, water, etc., she'd asked him to show her his collar. He'd blush and ask her not to make him do it. She'd merely tilt her head and wait patiently until he lowered his turtleneck to expose it. Once she gave him permission to cover the collar once more, he would pull her into his embrace. He didn't realize that she ensured no one else was privy to his actions or could see the collar. Though he was embarrassed, this game they played allowed him to become more confident in himself and accept his sexuality fully.

It's interesting that we often think men are comfortable with their sexuality when in actuality they can be just as uptight as women are—they just hide it better.

Public Humiliation

Public humiliation is very tricky. Some individuals will react poorly to it and others will be too shocked at first to know how to react at all. Those who get a thrill from being humiliated will see it as a reward. It's all in how it's handled. I'll provide some examples and leave the rest to you.

One couple I know used *Humiliation Play* in public at a grocery store. The male Dominant yelled at his female slave when she dropped some items on the floor. He was pretty loud about it and degraded her a bit. Needless to say, some onlookers including the store manager came to the female slave's rescue which the male Dominant used to his advantage by blaming her for upsetting the onlookers and making them think he was a bad man.

My major objection to this was that they engaged in *non-consensual* play with others as the onlookers and store manager didn't know the full scope of what was going on. But when you look at it objectively, this is no different than a woman yelling at her husband in public calling him a jerk because he didn't arrive at the restaurant on time and they lost their reservations. Or because he got lost and didn't follow the directions *she* told him to follow. You'll also notice that it's more acceptable and easier to overlook when a woman insults a man than the other way around. The next time you witness this behavior I'm sure you'll wonder if this interaction is as *vanilla* as you once thought.

Another great example of using public humiliation from a sexual perspective (on either a male or female) happened to a slave I saw at a club who'd been restrained and was being Flogged. The slave became very aroused as his Mistress stopped for a moment to run her hand over his back and buttocks. The slave began to gyrate his hips becoming more excited from the touch. The Mistress stepped back, stated loudly for all to hear; "What a whore you are getting excited from being Flogged." She then proceeded to Flog him even harder knowing that in his aroused state he could take more pain and that her words actually fueled his desire to suffer and endure more for her.

Sexual inspection

On a sexual level, for either gender, an inspection can be one of the most humiliating activities they undergo. The slave can be required to strip before the Dominant and show their body in complete nudity. Requiring them to remove everything including their socks and shoes even their jewelry will add an additional psychologically component as it tells them that they can't use anything to adorn themselves and physically strips them of all possessions. Thus they're standing before their Master/Mistress metaphorically and in actuality with nothing between "them". A very vulnerable experience!

The Master/Mistress can then take this sexual inspection one step further by circling the slave/submissive, commanding him to bend forward at the waist, as the Master/Mistress stands behind the slave. To add a deeper psychological/emotional component the slave can be ordered to spread their buttocks for the Master/Mistress to inspect their anus. Adding genitals inspections and commenting on it heightens the effect. The Master/Mistress can then take this inspection one step further commenting on the attributes or shortcomings of the slave's physique. The slave can also be required to strip in public and allow others to inspect him/her.

Gender Specific Humiliation

Though *Humiliation Play* can be performed on various levels and in various ways, and much of it is interchangeable between the genders, below are a few examples of how you can incorporate specific aspects which will increase the affect for either a man and woman and is gender specific. Though I will not create a scenario for each aspect, as I am confident you will have no trouble in creating them or incorporating these aspects into your novels, I will provide you with the information from a psychological perspective which I hope will provide you with a better understanding of how the humiliation will affect the individual and how best to use it in your plot and/or character development.

147

Humiliation Play is one of those things you negotiate and develop together. When using *Humiliation Play* you need to be specific. Some men and women like to be embarrassed in public not majorly at times but little things here and there. Some like to be cursed at and called names even told they're worthless so they can prove they're not or just feel comfortable in their own internalized concept of themselves.

For Women:

When playing with women, using humiliation in the areas of make-up, weight, sexual appeal, sexual exploits and sexual experiences will elicit very strong reactions. Below are a few examples. For the sake of simplicity, I will provide the examples as if you were doing them yourself.

Mess up a woman's make-up; drag your hand over her mouth and smear her lipstick then tell her she looks like a clown or worthless whore. If she cries drag your hand over her face and mess up her eye-make-up and mascara, even grab her by the hair and drag her before the mirror to show her how "ugly" she looks. That's very humiliating and degrading. From there you can go many places with your story.

Finding fault with the clothing she wears will elicit a strong emotional response. For instance: how her dress/slacks are too tight or too loose making her *look* like a whore or like a prude. Having your male character state that he wants someone who dresses to attract him not some "dumb bitch who can't even figure out what to wear", will put a serious spin on any relationship and have the reader sympathizing with your female character.

Sexual inadequacies are a major source of humiliation! You can have him attempt to degrade her by pointing out "how lousy she is at giving head" or how she just "lays there when he fucks her". And if you have her rationalize that she can't move because she's tied up, well doesn't that create another doorway for possibilities.

Humiliation can also be used to show the person's lack of participation as they're too shy to state what they like or how it feels when they're having sex providing their partner with feedback, even if it is just moaning or saying "it feels good". Or making her tell him how it feels to have him touch her, fuck her, put things inside her and get her to vocalize what she feels, then use it against her. For instance, telling her how wet and aroused she becomes when he's taking her, using her, even offering to give her to other men to use. The fact that her body is responding to the physical stimulus or sexual arouse he's perpetuating in her makes it difficult for her to deny the verbal accusations and/or connections he's making.

"I can feel how wet you are. You want me to let other men fuck you, don't you? Look how you tighten on my fingers just thinking about it."

You can even have the male Dominant drag his fingers coated with her desire over her face to mark her or have her smell and taste herself. (For men, making them taste their own essence then telling them how disgusting they look doing that and/or that even a woman doesn't swallow can be very humiliating and degrading.)

You can get as explicit as you desire and of course, I'm sure you can put flowery adjectives to my examples above. The point is humiliation can be used for or against the individual. And don't forget that within a sexual context using *dirty words* or being sexually explicit if acceptable however outside of it, it becomes mired and tainted with shame and guilt. These two conflicting emotions (desire and guilt) intensify the experience as her body and mind battle against each other. This internal battle is what will propel her into *subspace*. It's this conflict that will create the *short circuit,* if you will, that will push them over the edge into bliss or sexual release as their minds can't wrap around two conflicting realities

For Men

For males use their *machismo* and their desire to be brave against them. You can train them to take more pain or more *whatever* because it's for their Mistress/Master. When inflicting pain, make them count the strikes or how long they can endure a particular pressure of pain will make them accept more. Reinforcing the fact that a "real man" can take

149

10 seconds of a particular pain and *he* can only take four. If he cries out after ten lashes, tell him another slave took twenty; or better yet, remind him that he took twenty last week but is now too much of a weakling to handle the same amount. With men, playing with pain becomes a matter of encouragement and seducing them into taking more---and when all else fails, use their pride against them!

There was a slave I knew who had a Prince Albert piercing on his penis. His Mistress would use clothespins to pinch the skin underneath which is excruciatingly painful. Once she put the clothespin on, she'd tell him to count for her—1, 2, 3...counting slowly. She'd count with him. When he begged her to remove the clothespin because he couldn't take anymore, she would. She would brush against him softly and let him lean into her from his tied position letting him catch his breath for a moment. She'd whisper that he could do better and take more asking him if he wanted to please her; helping him—encouraging him—to take more—in essence seducing him into accepting the pain. He shored up his courage and they started again. When he insisted he couldn't go further, She would ask if he was a coward or tell him how disappointed she was that he wasn't as brave as she needed him to be or thought he was. This would motivate him into surrendering further—withstanding more. She got him to count slowly till 20 during their session. Afterward, she rewarded him for how brave he'd been and how proud she was of him for enduring so much for his Mistress.

***

There are so many more examples I can provide on various ways to incorporate *humiliation* into a relationship whether for fun or for *punishment*, however, at this point I'm sure you get the gist of it. Remember *humiliation* can be used just to tease the slave into pushing themselves further than what they thought they could endure and/or to elicit behavior modification, getting rid of the undesired behavior and attitudes.

It's imperative to realize that everyone has their own emotional connection to a particular activity, word, or act. It is those emotional connections which will deem the activity objectionable or acceptable. Where the activity is performed and whether it's in private or public, before a group of like minded individuals or a *vanilla* crowd, or whether it's perceived to be done in anger or affection will affect the person's acceptance of the same. Because of these varying factors, the slave's emotional reaction will vary from being embarrassed, humiliated, degraded or erotic. The conclusion will also be a big factor in this play.

For instance, after all is said and done, will the slave be rewarded or punished? And if humiliation was used as punishment, then the warning that if the behavior isn't corrected to the Master/Mistress' satisfaction further action will be taken or the slave might just be *dismissed* altogether! Sometimes the fear of *dismissal* more so than the pain of a severe *punishment* or *humiliation* is more frightening especially if their connection to the Dominant is strong as their standing in the household or their sense of *belonging* will be taken from them.

Remember, because of its emotional component humiliation will draw forth strong reactions. Ensure to incorporate whatever *Aftercare* is needed by the submissive/slave (and even the Dominant) to ensure future interactions and more importantly, a strengthening of the bond between the couple.

Chapter 9

What's it look like in writing?

Now that we've taken a look at the psychological components of dominance and submission as well as its dynamics and a variety of its vast potential and possibilities, let's look at the wording and how to bring the language of BDSM into your romance novels.

Words inspire action, loyalty, trust and surrender; thus, using them effectively is the difference between success and failure. Within the *Power Exchange* it's all in the wording as this is what will convey control, ownership, desire, and a whole host of other emotions as well as the lifestyle dynamics associate with Dominant and submissive interactions. Therefore, unlike with *vanilla* novels where everything is "flowery" and the adjectives are politically correct, and the action is sensual and passive, for BDMS romances you have to take a rougher more aggressive approach to your characters allowing the *naughty slut* as well as the *beast* free rein. Don't be afraid to use words such as slut, whore, cunt, dick or cock. The very fact that they're taboo is a delicious unconscious thrill in and of itself. It'll also shock your readers into reading more as they wonder what you'll do next.

Don't be afraid to show aggression or even controlled sadism in the Dominant—this is true to form. Yes, it is all about the Master/Mistress' desire and what they crave to share with their slave, just as it is about the need to belong and find that soulmate that will calm the chaos in a slave's heart and mind. Selfishness is ok! At times, even necessary in a BDSM relationship!

A word of advice when writing for your Dominant characters: you want Him/Her to speak with authority and assurance even when they are faced with an internal struggle of their own desire to push their submissive to the edge or when they fear their own Sadistic needs. Don't fall back on the old cliché of a Dominant screaming to get his/her way. The scariest Sadist I know actually speaks very softly making the slave become hyper-vigilant. It's when *She's* at Her cruelest that Her voice is sugary sweet.

Below are a few random examples of what these interactions look and sound like. I've also added a few examples of how Dominance is expressed in everyday activities and a few mock scenarios which I believe depict the *Power Exchange* between two Dominants, a Mistress and her slave, as well as a Master and his submissive. Feel free to change the genders around to suit your own tastes.

Meeting a slave's need for connection

Sir Jason and his slave have a specific type of attire—a uniform if you will—that they wear everyday which conveys their positions within his household. His slave loves to dress him. To accommodate her need, he dictates that she has to have his suits laid out at a specific time each morning and presented in a specific manner. This not only addresses her need to "dress him" to be fulfilled but also maintains the *Protocol* in their home of her serving him first thing in the morning.

Chivalry & Dominance

A way to show chivalrous activities while reinforcing a Dominant component in the mix is when he opens the door for her and allows her to walk in before him because it is a place He wishes her to enter. However, if he does not open the door for her she cannot enter and is not allowed in the establishment. Thus his allows her entry only to areas he desires her to be in. To the outside world he's being a gentleman. Within their dynamics, she realizes that she entered the establishment only because he allows it.

Another example occurs when the male slave will order for his Mistress at a restaurant after she has advised him what she desires to eat that night. It is then his duty and his responsibility to ensure the waiter provides her meal to her specifications.

<u>An individual's need to surrender</u>

The truth is I want to experience it all! To know what it's really like to surrender myself to another. To feel a man's control over my sexuality. To have him take pleasure in my body and draw forth my cries. To have a man who could withstand my strong personality and not cower before me but take all I have to offer and then demand more.

<u>Internal struggle:</u>

I'm embarrassed. Scared. Concerned. Immature. Pissed. Full of hope. And yet, confused and confident all at the same time. Should I be so honest? Or should I pretend as I've done for years, as many others have done hoping no one will notice and they'll be able to continue. Embarrassed to admit what I yearn for.

Below are a few vignettes showing the *Power Exchange* as it is portrayed within actual interactions between a Master/Mistress and their slaves. It goes without saying that the genders in each *Scene* are interchangeable.

The Club

I had upset you but this wasn't about punishment, it was about Ownership and you made your position on that fact abundantly clear. To my surprise you stopped before a Spanking bench and told me to lean over it. I rarely played in public and never as a submissive and was reluctant to do so now. I gasped as you grabbed my hair and thrust me forward not giving me any further say. Your elbow pressed into my spine, pinning me over the bench. You didn't tie my hands or restrain me in any way, just warned me not to make any attempts at covering myself. You grabbed my skirt and yanked it up then quickly pulled my underwear to my knees. I felt the color raise in my cheeks more and more as I heard the crowd gathering. I couldn't believe you were actually doing this before everyone and pushed against the Spanking bench to stand, to cover myself, to save some of my dignity.

You tighten the hold in my hair making me cry out, pinning me with your body, holding me in place. "You will receive 20 lashes and you will count them out. Every time you miss a count or attempt to cover yourself, we'll start the count again."

I'd heard that tone in your voice before. I knew you wouldn't waver. I winced as you tightened your hand in my hair prompting my answer. "Fine," I yelled angrily refusing to be humiliated further by arguing.

Slowly you unbuckled your belt and pulled it from its loops and doubled it over. I thought I'd been ready for the first impact but I wasn't and jumped when I felt the sharp sting against my bare ass cheeks. "One." I gritted between my teeth and waited for the next one.

"That's not how you were taught to count, Jessie."

You already knew my stubborn streak had kicked in and raised the belt again, landing it across my cheeks. "Two. Three. Four." I counted them off.

Your hand tightened in my hair once again, pulling my head back as you whispered in my ear, repeating your words once more. "That's not how you were taught to count, Jessie." I growled at you in response and you grinned. "Have it your way."

You pushed me back down, stepped back, and raised the belt choosing your target. The back of my thighs. My left buttock—my right. The force always the same. The leather biting into my tender flesh. I could feel the heat rising, each strike compounded by the one before, making me tremble as the pain of it washed over me. You raised your hand another five times and waited for the proper count and still I refused. You raised the belt again another three before leaning into me once more. Your hand soothing over my burning cheeks; that more than anything else broke through my stubbornness and made me whimper softly.

"You know I will do this all night until you have counted properly, my sweet whore." You placed a tender kiss against my cheek, my temple. Your words whispered for my ears alone.

"Why...why are you doing this?" My voice was hoarse from biting back tears.

Your hand loosened from my hair and slid over my neck, your fingers spreading out over the delicate skin of my throat—tightening. Your mouth against my ear, "You belong to me, Jessie. Anytime. Anywhere. Anyway I desire."

It was that simple!

I knew you didn't need an answer but nodded anyway, "Yes, Sir."

I could feel the tears I'd held back rolling down my cheeks. You licked one, then another and pressed your body against mine. I could feel your arousal. Feel your Ownership as your hand squeezed slightly against my throat, feeling me swallow.

Your lips brushed softly against my ear once again, "Count for me, Jessie. Count for us!"

I felt a sob wrenched from my throat at your solemn request as I realized your need was just as strong as mine.

I missed the feel of your body covering mine the minute you stood up straight once more. Your hand returned to my hair, your grip not as painful yet controlling all the same. You raised the belt once more and it landed with the same harsh impact as the other twelve had. My body trembled absorbing each strike as I began to count for you.

"One...Master."

My Mistress' Mark

I could see my reflection in the glass window before me as lightening streaked across the sky. The marks Mistress carved into my flesh the night before became visible as lightening lit the room. The ropes held me against the straight-backed chair. My arms bound to the wooden spokes of the chair—you always enjoyed leaving my chest exposed to your view. My legs were spread wide, anchored to the chair legs. My cock pulsed against the harsh material of the denim jeans I wore and though I tried to shift slightly to give it some relief, I could barely move an inch. It would suffer until you were ready to call it forth.

Your voice was a soft erotic seduction, the prelude to your cruelty as you breathed against my ear, causing the hairs at the back of my neck to rise. "I want to taste, baby. I have to taste your essence once more."

Without further words, you brought your hand down hard over the initials you'd carved into my chest the night before, slapping at it once, twice, and then again, until the thin scab that had formed to heal my tender flesh lost its hold and a few thin drops of blood emerged in its place.

My groans were lost in the trio of thunder claps that echoed around us as if the storm itself kept pace with your actions. My back arched to lessen the pain but that only trapped me further against the chair and your blade. I turned my face into the crook of your neck as you leaned forward over my shoulder.

I felt your thighs brush against my fingers and I reached for you, needing to anchor myself if only with a touch of your flesh. The salt from your fingertips as you rubbed them over my skin stung yet it was the reverent way you gathered the drops of blood on your fingertips then took them to your mouth for a taste, and the sensual way your tongue come forth to lick along the edge of your fingertips, that left me breathless, drawing a moan from my lips as I stared up at you.

"This is mine, Michael. Whatever I call forth from you belongs to me!"

With those words, you drew your fingers into your mouth and sucked hungrily. Your eyes seemed to darken from their intensity as you looked down at me.

Your hand rose once more and I turned my head to the other side to give you ample room, already knowing what you would do. I tried to keep my body relaxed and not anticipate the strikes as they flew against my chest knowing if I tensed it would merely make the slaps more painful. I turned my face into your shoulder and bit softly, breathing through my mouth. My chest rose and fell—my heartbeat pounding. I couldn't help the groan that escaped my lips as each slap built on the one before it intensifying the stringing sensation until it became a burn than actual pain.

Once again you ran your fingers over my tender flesh, leaving your sting behind as you moistened your fingertips with my blood. The initials you'd carved wept my blood in tiny little drops down my chest. I heard you groan as your mouth nibbled hard over my ear, my neck, your words sending a craving so intense through me I felt my knees give way and was pleased to be sitting down or I might have embarrassed myself.

"I need more, Michael. I have to have more…so much more", you growled and dragged the knife blade over my chest, along my collarbone, over my jugular then lower once more before nicking my flesh and drawing forth what you craved most. I held my breath as I watched you lean forward, your tongue brushing sensually along my flesh, tasting each drop before covering your mark with your mouth and feeding on me.

I could do nothing but surrender!

Everything I was belonged to you.

Everything I had was yours to take.

You hungered—and I fed you!

And with that feeding, I lost myself to you forever. My body's explosive release told you just how much your words and feeding affected me and how my own need—my own cravings—matched yours!

The Shower

I stood under the shower, rinsing the shampoo from my hair, rubbing at my eyes to get the soap out of them then turning my face up to the warm water once more. I gasped as a hand grip my hair. I thought I was alone in the house. You tightened your grip, forcing my face to remain looking up, the water cascading over my eyes, nose and mouth, making it hard for me to breathe. I spit out the water as it entered my mouth each time I tried to take a breath. I felt your free hand cover my left breast. My heartbeat pounding beneath. Then your body pressed against mine. I felt your cock between my round cheeks and I couldn't help but press back against you.

"You trust me don't you, baby?"

"Yes." My words were garbled from talking through the water. Goose bumps emerging all over my body at your words despite the warmth of the water at your words.

You ordered me to place my hands against the shower wall before me and arch my body, then you maneuvered the showerhead to allow the water to fall straight down over my back. Your feet kicked at mine, widening them. Your hand still gripped my hair, letting me pull out of the cascading water for a moment to breathe fully again. I felt my heart pound against my chest. Not sure what to expect. I scream in surprise and pain as I felt the sting of the leather slap over my ass cheeks making me jump only to hear your sadistic chuckle.

Again and again I felt the belt come down over my ass warming it, your hand in my hair, pulling my face constantly back under the water despite my struggles, keeping it there as the lashes grew harder and harder. The water adding to the stinging sensation. Its little droplets were like pinpricks as the belt claimed more and more of my flesh. I cried out in pain over and over begging, pleading for you to stop...for you to keep going. Needing your sadism. Feeling it calming the chaos inside me that had been building for the past week. My body began to tremble uncontrollably as you worked the belt up and down my back, my shoulders, my ass, pulling me under the water repeatedly making me gasp for breath.

I screamed out, unable to take anymore, and you pressed your body against mine, shielding me from the water, wrapping your arms around me. I cried against you and heard your words of comfort slowly penetrate the haze of pain...of pleasure...at being used so severely. Your words spoke of pride in *your property*, your loving whore, whispering your desire, your joy at owning me. You spoke of your need to hear my screams, your joy of holding my trembling body against yours.

"Hold me...please...please don't let go. Please don't let go." My words were a desperate plea repeated over and over as I melted into your embrace. Your body my only connection to reality and I knew I'd be lost without your arms anchoring me to you.

"I won't let go, baby. I won't let go of my sweet slave. You belong to me! You belong to me, my love." Your words were a mere whisper against my ear as they penetrated the haze of pain and pleasure. I felt your hand slide down my body. Your fingers spreading, squeezing, exploring my tender flesh. Your hand made its way lower to brush over my clit. Stroking me intimately. I could feel you bite my back, my shoulders. Your cock hard, nestled between my round cheeks. My body trembled anew as pleasure mixed with pain until my body shattered under your encouragement. Your arms around me the only thing holding me up as my legs gave way. Then your hand was in my hair, turning my face back to cover my mouth with yours, drinking the sounds of my ecstasy.

***

As with any novel you write whether mainstream *vanilla* or BDSM, one rule will always remain the same, if it doesn't excite you, it won't excite your readers. Ensure to incorporate the six senses: sight, sound, smell, touch, tastes and most important of all the emotional connection which will help guide your reader in the intricate world of dominance and submission. It is the affection within the sadism that is at the heart of every *Power Exchange* and BDSM relationship; and it is this mixture of affection and pain that creates and feeds the erotic sensual needs of both the Dominant and the submissive.

Chapter 10

BDSM for Writers Checklist

The thing to remember about the *BDSM for Writers Checklist* is that anything and everything can be added to it. From domestic activities (such as cooking and cleaning), to fetishes, to sexual activities, and service oriented issues. The list is forever expanding as you and your relationship grows—as your characters' relationship grows. As the Master/Mistress, you can add what's most important to you. The things you don't desire should remain on the list since it allows the submissive/slave to know what's not acceptable.

I recommend completing a new *BDSM for Writers Checklist* for every significant character in your novel and a different one if you're writing a second novel with the same characters as you will find dramatic changes in behavior and tolerance. Plus it may give you ideas to further your character development, scenes, even possible plot changes. And of course, things the submissive/slave doesn't like are wonderful tools to use when *Punishing* them. More importantly, it will help you create the psychological make-up and the inner fortitude of your characters and show their willingness to surrender and/or dominate.

Though in general a *BDSM Checklist* is often completed only by the slave/submissive to allow the Dominant to assess the slave's experience and willingness to explore, I believe that the Dominant should also complete their own list as it's important for the one that yields the Whip to know their own limits. And of course as you're developing a character profile for your novel, you'll want to know what traits each significant character will have.

Please note for the sake of simplicity I will fluctuate between addressing you as the Dominant and referring information for your characters. I believe this will help you internalize the information provided and help you get a better perspective of the essence of the *Power Exchange.*

As a writer, the list will provide you with wonderful ideas that you can incorporate into your scenes as well as help you build the psychological profile of your characters. Noticing what activities are desirable or acceptable and when, will not only outline a particular erotic scene but will also provide you with ideas on coercion, affection, and consensual non-consensual activities to conduct. Though remember what's acceptable in fiction can get you tossed in jail in real-life or ostracized from some places and ruin your reputation.

Another thing to keep in mind is that what a person will do or explore will continuously change as they grow in experience, self-confidence and in the trust they share with another person. Thus what one of your characters may be willing to do with *Tom*, she/he would never do with *Harry*.

The *BDSM for Writers Checklist* I've created also provides a place to note any medical issues, phobias, or physical limitations which will greatly affect how an individual—whether Dominant or submissive/slave—will be able to interact with others. For instance, if the slave has diabetes or circulatory problems, prolonged bondage is something you want to keep a close eye on to ensure there are no blood flow restrictions, something that can become life threatening or result in serious physical and medical consequences. You'd also want to ensure you know if the person takes insulin and when they last eat to ensure they have the stamina for *Play* and that you know what you should do if they become disoriented or faint. Also, if a person has claustrophobia, putting them in a cage or even tying them up and placing them in a closet may exacerbate this condition and make them violent or withdrawn even cause a psychotic break. As you are realizing, there's more to Dominating/Mastering another individual than merely knowing how to throw a Whip.

My personal favorite question in the *BDSM for Writers Checklist* is the question of *"Force"*. This is a major psychological and emotional window into the individual. Would the submissive/slave accept any activity he/she previously stated as a *"Limit"* if *"Force"* were involved? You might find that, given a choice, the individual would set a Limit for themselves out of their cultural or societal norms; however, they would leave it up to their Master's discretion and feel comfortable with the activity because they "had no choice" and they would do it only to "please their Master."

Please note, when I refer to *Force* in this context, I am in no way suggesting the slave/submissive would desire an unknown assailant to *force* them into conducting or participating in any of these activities. This would be a crime! I am specifically referring to a trusted Master/Mistress whom the submissive/slave knows and trusts and therefore he/she would be willing to experience these more frightening activities from a consensual standpoint.

Though all *BDSM Checklists* are different, below is the simplest way I know how to address the multitude of possibilities. Splitting the list into what the individual has done and what he/she would like to do is the first step. Once they've revealed this information (or you've outlined it for your character), it's a matter of determining desires, limits, and whether they'd like to give up total control or be *Forced* into doing so. Also, it's important to remember that modifications will play a major role into whether a person will accept an activity or not. Remember the example I previously gave about someone accepting a Spanking with an opened hand but not with an instrument. And of course, those things they *hate* are always a sinfully wicked activity to use when you need to *Punish* the slave/submissive or you desire to reinforce your *Ownership*.

Don't forget *Force* is a major turn-on! What a slave/submissive won't do willingly by choice they may do if required or *forced* to do so by their Master/Mistress. It's that little voice inside saying, "I had no choice in the matter, Master/Mistress, *forced* me to…" This literally creates a free pass for the individual to be naughty—slutty—a whore! The use of *force* gives the slave/sub the ability to overcome their bias, fears, and societal norms and surrender completely. It's like saying, "The Devil made me do it." And we all know that makes being "bad" deliciously sweeter. Plus, it's a wonderful excuse…isn't it?

I've also broken down the *BDSM for Writers Checklist* into various types of activities, to include not only what they've experienced and what they'd like to experience but also the various categories of activities which include: service, physical, sexual, *Edge Play* and *Force*. Each activity can be further broken down into specifics; however that would make this *BDSM Checklist* at least 10 to 20 pages long.

For example: service can be alone or with others present; for the Master or for someone designated by the Master; in uniform or naked. Sex can be further broken down by using protection such as condoms, with designated individuals, with strangers, as well as in public or private. Remember, that the individual may be willing to behave a certain way in private surrendering to the Master/Mistress however in public the individual would buck at such interactions. Therefore I'll merely leave room for you to be more specific and/or add anything else you'd like.

Below are a few examples to get you started in understanding the vast dynamics disclosed from a simple *BDSM Checklist* and the importance of information you can gain from it.

Example of a slave's response to *BDSM Checklist for Writers*

Character Name: Zachary   **BDSM Identity:** slave
Date: December 10, 2010   **Initial List**: Yes
Limits: Monogamy –no same sex contacts –condom sex __ only_____
Medical conditions: Right knee surgery September 5, 2010 can't kneel long periods. ___ Asthma. _____

Emergency contacts/measures needed: _Use Inhaler if I experience an Asthma attack._____
Phobias: terrified of dogs_____
Other issues: none_____

Rating:

1. Love it
2. Hate it
3. Want to try
4. It's ok—Take it/Leave it
5. Force (will accept if desired/forced by Master/Mistress)
6. Need Modifications (Explain)
7. Never/again—Hard Limit

Activity	Have Experienced					Want to Experience				
	Giving	Receiving	Yes	No	Rate	Giving	Receiving	Yes	No	Rate
Massage	X	X	X		1	X	X	X		1
Spanking		X	X		2		X		X	2
Whips Single-tail				X	1		X	X		1
Kneeling	X		X		1	X		X		5/6
Anal Sex	X		X		1		X	X		1
Same Gender Sex				X	5				X	5
Serving Maid/butler	X		X		1	X		X		1
Cross-dressing				X	7				X	7

Explanations to items noted above needing modifications:

a. Kneeling: i will kneel as Mistress/Master requires. i humbly ask that i be allowed to use a pillow as it is difficult to kneel for periods longer than one hour.

b. Inhale: my inhaler is in my coat pocket. If I have difficulty breathing, giving me two puffs will alleviate the problem.

Let's take a look at Zachary's list. He identifies as a slave and it's understood that most of what he has experienced or will experience will be at the direction/discretion of his Master/Mistress. And though he stated no "same sex contact", this doesn't mean he wouldn't submit to a male Dominant or engage in sexual activities with him since he also indicated that he wanted to experience same sex activities if #5—*Forced.*

Zachary is service oriented and loves giving massages and serving as butler. We can also assume that he is versed with the typical protocols of a slave such as kneeling before his Master/Mistress. We immediately note what his *Limits* as well as his phobias are, yet more importantly, that he has had surgery and he has asthma which requires an inhaler. Therefore, the Dominant should ensure that before any interactions are engaged in, She/He knows where that inhaler is. It would also be good to have an extra one designated only for the Play Room or in the Toy Bag to ensure it's always available as this is a matter of life and death.

Knowing whether the slave/sub likes an activity or not will give you some insight into his level of surrender and whether he's an alpha slave or needs a strict hand. The fact that Zachary "loves" kneeling shows he enjoys showing his Master/Mistress respect and surrendering completely. However as you can see, he also stated he would allow his Master/Mistress to *Force* him to kneel. Though at first this may be confusing, it's really not when you take into consideration the fact that he's had surgery on his right knee and this can cause physical pain and even re-injury depending on how far into his recovery he is. You'll also notice that he stated he would *Want to Experience* if he was #5—*Forced* and #6—Modificiations were made. At the bottom of the checklist he stipulated what these modifications were. And if they're not there, the Dominant can include them as she/he reviews the checklist with Zachery and makes her/his own notations.

It should be noted that most slaves will want to please their Master/Mistress and will endure pain and discomfort for them. However it is the Master/Mistress' responsibility to keep the slave's well-being upper most in mind and deny them this privilege until it will not cause them harm. An ethical Master/Mistress would forego a slave's kneeling until recovery was complete and provide him with an alternative to kneeling such as standing with his head bowed and his hands behind his back. Or if kneeling causes only minor discomfort, the Master/Mistress may choose to *force* him to do so while providing a pillow for him on which to kneel on and limiting the time spent kneeling. For example: 10 minutes instead of a half hour. Modifications can also be made to the kneeling position as he can be allowed to lean back and rest on his feet instead which would take the strain off the knee as opposed to kneeling straight up which puts all the pressure directly on the knees itself. And there are knee pads which the slave can wear to minimize/eliminate the pressure on the knees. (These pads are the same worn by tile installers and rescue workers and can be purchased for $20 or so at most hardware stores or sporting goods stores.)

As we continue our review of Zachary's character based on his responses, you'll notice the *BDSM for Writers Checklist* shows that Zachary #2—**hates** Spankings but would tolerate them at his Master/Mistress' choice. This is wonderful information to know as you now have a tool to use when administering *Punishment* or should you decide to torture/torment him in a *Scene* just for your Sadistic pleasure. When you limit yourself to using the things he hates for *Punishment* it reinforces your control as he would be unlikely to transgress in such a manner again any time in the near future. And the Spanking (the activity he hates) becomes one which he'll associate with humiliation thus further reinforcing your Dominant character's control.

It's also important to know what activities he's experienced from the position of giving as opposed to receiving. Not only will this tell you whether or not his inclinations are those of a Dominant/Switch/slave/submissive but also what his role has been in the process. For instance, Zachary states he has experienced "giving" anal sex and loves it. However he has not experienced it himself as "receiving" was blank, but he would like to experience "receiving". An important discovery here is that he rated the activity of *Want to Experience* "receiving" as #1—Love it. This reveals that he has fantasized about receiving anal sex and "loves" the idea. Therefore, he would be receptive to the same. Now don't forget, just because he loved something in theory/fantasy doesn't mean he'll enjoy it after trying it. His next *BDSM Checklist* might reflect that he's experienced receiving anal sex and hated it and has even placed it on his limits list.

If we continue along the anal sex path, connecting what we already know about Zachary with what else is possible, you find that he has never experienced same gender sex but is willing to try the same if #5—*Forced*. This opens the door to many erotically enticing *Scenes* and ways to mentally torment him or excite him with the idea.

More importantly, the fact that he would accept it if *forced* states two things: (1) he would surrender all to his Master/Mistress; and (2) he wants to be able to bypass the guilt associated with the activity. And though you notice in the "Limits" section that he stated "no same sex contacts", he also stated he'd want to experience it if forced. Thus, this is something to discuss beforehand. This is an excellent example of *consensual non-consensuality.*

As we continue with our review, you'll notice one of his #7—**Hard Limits** is Crossdressing. This *Hard Limit* is something which is honored. You can tease him about it, but never cross the line or you'll destroy trust and of course it stops being consensual and crosses into abuse.

As you review the *BDSM for Writers Checklist* for the slave/submissive, you'll want to notice if the individual is leaving every decision up to the Master/Mistress. This can be a sign of complete surrender which is wonderful; however, it can also be a sign of someone who wants to take no responsibility for their actions and these slaves/submissives will become a source of frustration to the Master/Mistress. Though it's great to have a slave who surrenders completely, it's boring to have one that gives you no input and thus doesn't give you the feedback you need to "push against" to challenge you to be a better Dominant and/or give you that thrill of having really pushed your slave/submissive into another level of physical/sexual surrender.

Let's take a look at one more example; this time from the Dominant's perspective. When developing your character you'll want to use what the Dominant likes and how she/he identifies as a way to not only build erotic scenes but also their personality. You'll notice if they enjoy more of the *Edge Play* scenarios and if they've actually experienced them. Sometimes loving them and experiencing them from a Master/Mistress perspective is not about fear of trying, but fear of releasing that "*Beast*" within and not being confident enough with yourself that you'll be able to keep control of it. This internal struggle with the "*Beast Within*" is not only a great character identifier but also something you can use for/or against the Dominant as you develop his/her character and interactions with others since some people may see the "Beast" within the Dominant and others never get that privilege. As I previously discussed, some women struggle with their desire for control and sadism as society has taught them women should never behave that way.

Example of a Master/Mistress response to
BDSM for Writers Checklist

Character Name: Jessica
BDSM Identity: Mistress/Sadist
Date: April 6, 2010
Initial List: 3-years experience
Limits: Men
Medical conditions: None
Emergency contacts/measures needed: Josh (212) 555-xxxx friend, fellow Dominant
Phobias: Heights
Other issues: none

Rating:
1. Love it
2. Hate it
3. Want to try
4. It's ok—Take it/Leave it
5. Force (will accept if desired/forced by Master/Mistress)
6. Need Modifications (Explain)
7. Never/again—Hard Limit

Have Experienced   Want to Experience

Activity	Giving	Receiving	Yes	No	Rate	Giving	Receiving	Yes	No	Rate
Spanking	X				2					2
Caning	X				1	X				1
Kneeling		X			1		X			1
Anal Sex	X						X			3
Same Gender Sex					7					7
Whips Single-tail	X				1	X				1
Knife Play	X				1	X				1
Fire Play	X	X			1/6	X				1/6
Breath Play	X				1	X				1
Orgasm Denial	X	X			1	X	X			1
Threesome Female, male, male					1					1/7

Explanations to items noted above needing modifications:

a. Fire Play: Josh should be present as am still learning

b. Hard Limit: Male Dom can have his female slave present in the room during the

Threesome however she can observe only. (Note: When playing with Josh, we can

have his slave tied to the wall and forced to watch. Josh enjoys torturing her that way.)

As you review Mistress Jessica's *BDSM Checklist for Writers* you'll notice that she's been in the *Scene* for three years at minimum. You see she has no medical conditions and her only phobia is heights. You notice that she identified as a Dominant and a Sadist. She provided a contact number for a friend and specified him as a *kink friendly* individual and fellow Dominant thus if there are any problems, the person calling can be open and honest about the situation.

As you beginning to go down her *BDSM Checklist* you may be surprised to see that she indicated Spanking was #2—Hates it but Caning was #1—Love it. Though this may seem as a contradiction since the activities of Spanking and Caning are very similar and both incorporate the buttocks, it's important to remember that the emotional connection to each is different and thus it's not unusual to dislike one activity and love another similar one.

As her self-identity in the lifestyle goes, she enjoys the more sadistic sides of BDSM and has experience with it. She did note under *Fire Play* that she #1—Loves it and had #6—Modification necessary for it. As you review her explanation, she states she'd like her Dominant friend Josh to be present as she's still learning.

As you continue to review her list, you'll notice that *giving* anal sex is something she #1—Loves it, however, she has not personally experienced it but would like to try it. It shouldn't surprise you that woman enjoy *giving* anal sex since this is one of the most taboo riddled activities there is in both the BDSM and *vanilla* realms. It is also a tremendous score of power and is often viewed as the ultimate surrender of a slave to his/her Master/Mistress. The fact that Mistress Jessica wants to experience it with her slave shows her trust in him and perhaps a desire to intensify their emotional connection.

As you continue to review her sexual exploits and desires, you'll learn that she #1—Love it for Orgasm Denial both *giving* and *receiving*. Now this will immediately identify her as sensually driven as she would enjoy bringing her slave/submissive to a level of sexual need and frustration and keep him peaking before allowing him to reach his climax. The fact that she enjoys it herself merely helps to heighten the

173

pleasure she derives in sexually tormenting her slave. This is also a wonderful characteristic to have in your character development as it shows her ability to be patient enough to drive them both to erotic heights. Then again, you could always wonder just who is enforcing *Orgasm Denial* on her? Is she using her slave to heighten her desire, denying herself the ability to reach release or is she craving her slave's touch and denying herself the same until she pushes him so far that he shows her the *beast within* himself satisfying them both. And let's not forget that *Orgasm Denial* is a wonderful *Punishment* to use on a slave.

You'll also notice that Mistress Jessica has a *Hard Limit* on same sex interactions between herself and another woman. However, she does not appear to have the same *Hard Limit* when it comes to her male slave interacting with another male as she enjoys threesomes. Keep in mind that her participation in a threesome does not indicate that she will permit her slave to interact sexually with another male, just that she enjoys interacting with two men simultaneously. You will also notice that she has made modifications in her *Hard Limits* to allow the presence of another woman who is bound and only able to observe but not participate in her interactions. Perhaps this is a sign of her not wanting another woman to touch her slave.

As you've noticed, there are vast quantities of data that you can attain from a simple *BDSM for Writers Checklist* not only from a physical and medical perspective but even more so from a psychological and emotional perspective as well.

Each list will vary depending on the identity of the person and whether they identify as Master/Mistress, Dominant, Switch, slave, submissive, Sadist or merely a *Kinkster*. And of course, men and women will have their own particulars as well with their own emotional, cultural, religious and spiritual connections.

For a surprising twist, I would encourage you to complete a *BDSM for Writers Checklist* for one of your characters (or all) merely checking boxes and completing the information. Afterward you can further develop their character traits around the *BDSM Checklist*. You may be surprised at the complexity of your characters and the amazing storyline that develops.

In real life, I recommend everyone complete this or a similar BDSM Checklist at least every six-months or at minimum once as year. It not only reminds you of what you've done and may want to improve upon, but it also shows you where you may be stuck and how you want to expand and explore, even if it's with a friend present while with your slave and/or Master/Mistress.

Feel free to make copies of the *BDSM for Writers Checklist* in this book for your personal use and/or purchase a set of the specially designed *BDSM for Writers Checklist* Packets. (Also available online at www.bdsmforwriters.com.)

Remember every activity, whether physical or sexual, can be further broken down into specifics such as Spanking with your hand, Spanking with a hair brush, Spanking over-the-knee, etc. Get as specific as you want to as you create your romance novels. Feel free to add any activities you wish your character(s) to perform that aren't on the list. You might even find that you save some activities for specific characters; and, as you grow in your comfort with creating and writing BDSM romances your characters will explore more of these wonderfully erotic and sometimes intense and dangerous activities.

Feel free to use the *BDSM for Writers Checklist* I've created to help you with character development and to give you ideas on what deviously wicked scenes you can come up with, not to mention all those sinfully erotic predicaments you can have your characters experience. Sometimes, you can develop your character profile based on the responses you've outlined in the *BDSM Checklist,* discovering your character as he/she reveals themselves to you.

When using the *BDSM Checklist for Writers* for your character(s) development, you may want to create different lists depending on the various other characters your main protagonist interacts with. For example, just because your heroine is completely open with her slave doesn't mean she will be open with a new love interest who may happen to be another Dominant or even another slave. And of course, if you're making a sequel to your book, you may find that in book number two or three, your character(s) have grown and are much more daring and sexually inventive, or they may have regressed as they struggle with issues of their self-acceptance or because of a traumatic experience. Perhaps a slave she/he was playing with died, or she/he lost custody of their child, or is denied family connections because of her/his participation in this lifestyle. These issues would change a person. Not that you wouldn't have the desires, but that you might not act upon them—isn't this a great plot for a story as well!

I hope the *BDSM for Writers Checklist* I've created helps you in writing your BDSM romances, suspense, horror novels and in any other genre you write in. Remember there's much more you can add to it and of course, feel free to do so.

BDSM for Writers Checklist
Character Development

Character Name: _____

BDSM Identity: _____

Date: _____Initial List/Subsequent:_____

Limits:_____
_____
_____

Medical conditions:_____
_____

Emergency contacts/measures needed: _____
_____
_____

Phobias: _____
_____
_____

Other issues: _____
_____

> **Rating:**
> 1. Love it
> 2. Hate it
> 3. Want to try
> 4. It's ok—Take it/Leave it
> 5. Force (will accept if desired/forced by Master/Mistress)
> 6. Need Modifications (Explain)
> 7. Never/again—Hard Limit

	Have Experienced					Want to Experience				
Activity	Giving	Receiving	Yes	No	Rate	Giving	Receiving	Yes	No	Rate
Services										
Collars										
Gags										
Kneeling										
Blindfolds										
Restricted eye contract										
Protocols										
Rituals										
Butler/Maid										
Sissy Maid										
Foot worship										
Feminization										

Activity	Have Experienced					Want to Experience				
	Giving	Receiving	Yes	No	Rate	Giving	Receiving	Yes	No	Rate
Sexual Activities										
Sex (without condom)										
Vaginal										
Fellatio										
Cunnilingus										
Anal										
Rimming										
CBT (Cock & Ball Torment)										
Strap-on										
Same Gender										
Rape (consensual)										
Threesome (female, male, male)										
Threesome (female, female, male)										
Sex with strangers										
Gang bang										
Forced orgasm										

Activity	Have Experienced					Want to Experience				
	Giving	Receiving	Yes	No	Rate	Giving	Receiving	Yes	No	Rate
Roleplaying										
Religious Scenes										
Torture Scenes										
Vampire Scenes										
Predicament Bondage										
Age Play (consenting adults)										
Daddy/little girl										
Puppy Play										
Pony Play										
Prisoner/Warden										
Boss/secretary										

	Have Experienced						Want to Experience				
Activity	Giving	Receiving	Yes	No	Rate		Giving	Receiving	Yes	No	Rate
Restraints (any kind)											
Metal Handcuffs											
Rope Bondage											
Flogging											
Whips Single Tail											
Whips--other											
Nipple Clamps											
Spanking											
Spanking (over-the-knee)											
Spanking (Implement)											
Caning											
Chastity Training/Control											
Medical Scenes											
Needle Play											
Videotaping											
Mummification											

Activity	Have Experienced						Want to Experience				
	Giving	Receiving	Yes	No	Rate		Giving	Receiving	Yes	No	Rate
Humiliation Public											
Humiliation Private											
Suspension											
Sensory Deprivation											
Predicament Bondage											
Orgasm Denial											
Crossdressing											
Physical/ Restraints											
Bondage											
Hogtied											
Straight Jacket											
Chains											
Movement restriction											
Cages											

Have Experienced   Want to Experience

Activity	Giving	Receiving	Yes	No	Rate	Giving	Receiving	Yes	No	Rate
Edge Play										
Breath Restriction										
Fire play										
Inverted Suspension										
Abduction scenes										
Blood Play										
Branding										
Electrical Shock										
Urethral Sounds										
Fisting										
Knife Play										

Activity	Have Experienced						Want to Experience				
	Giving	Receiving	Yes	No	Rate		Giving	Receiving	Yes	No	Rate
Mind Fucks											
Interrogations											
Fear Play											
Phobia Play											
Hypnosis											
Force											
Same Gender Sex											
Waterboarding/ Drowning											
Anything else											

Explanations to items noted above needing modifications:

_____
_____
_____
_____
_____
_____
_____
_____

Other issues which could affect interactions:
(medical/physical/emotional/past-history)

_____
_____
_____
_____
_____
_____
_____
_____

Possible interactions with others/strangers:

_____
_____
_____
_____
_____
_____

Deliciously wicked thoughts to try:

_____
_____
_____
_____
_____

Anything else/Comments:

_____

_____

_____

_____

_____

_____

Notes/Thoughts:

Chapter 11

Resources

Below I've listed a few resources for you to explore not only from the perspective of reading materials which will aid in your research and understanding of this uniquely complex lifestyle but also a few mass market videos that will help you see how the concepts of BDSM are portrayed in a semi-positive light.

I have also provided you with the names of some of great organizations within the BDSM community which yield a lot of valuable information both in education and legal issues. Though I don't have the room to list every organization in the country, I have referenced some of the ones on the East Coast I know personally and have worked with at times. For organizations in your area, review the Internet. You should be able to discover some in your local vicinity. Sometimes the closest one to you may be an hour or two away. It's worth taking the time to seek them out.

If you're interested in learning about BDSM and participating in some fun and informative workshops combined with a safe and discreet place to learn and/or *Play*; indulging your voyeuristic tendencies as you build up your courage; or merely want to allow your curiosity a little taste of a few activities, research the Internet for local groups in your area and their upcoming events.

If you're adventurous and would like to attend a four day or week long function, below are a few major events (on the East Coast) that you can easily find on the Internet which will provide you with hours/days of fun: Floating World (New Jersey), Dark Odyssey (Washington, DC), TESFest (New York City/New Jersey), and Shibari Con (Chicago).

Texas has several well known organizations that hold yearly events in Dallas, Austin and Houston. There's even a "*Male Slave Hunt*" planned by one organization I know of. I'm not sure if it's true that they grow everything bigger in Texas but I'll have to participate and better in Texas. Think I'll have to participate in that *"Male Slave Hunt"* just to be sure. And wouldn't that be a wonderful story to tell and read!

Most of these Events have *"Open Play Areas"*—dungeons which are equipped with various different equipment for your enjoyment. There are always cleaning stations in the Dungeon which hold accessories such as anti-bacterial wipes and pads to use on tables, even condoms and lube as some sexual activities are permissible. The equipment in most of these events includes a variety of Crosses, Spanking Benches, metal cages, A-frames where you can tie your slave/submissive, designated rope play areas, including *Fire Play* areas, and *Needle Play* stations, etc.

Open Play Areas means you can *Play* in the public Dungeon they've created for the event after the workshops or during open Dungeon hours. There's always something or someone to watch and if you have questions or want to try something new or merely practice throwing a Whip or try your hand at bondage, there's typically someone who's willing to help.

Most of the events have begun to offer additional areas specifically designated for a particular gender or sexual orientation groups. For example: the event may have a "Men's Only" Play Room, a "Lesbian Only" or a "Transgender Only" play room, along with the *Open Play Areas* where anyone can play regardless of gender or sexual orientation. These areas are not segregated because of any disparagement to the group. They are actually provided at the request of these groups who have some members who feel more comfortable playing among individuals with the same sexual orientation and gender identity as themselves.

These events are reasonably priced and closed off to the public once registration capacity is met. Therefore you don't need to fear that someone will walk in from the street and gawk at you. And if you do bump into a neighbor or co-worker at the event, rest assured that they're there for the same reasons you are. So either say hello or stay at the other end of the Dungeon.

There are of course dozens of events each year throughout the United States held in hotels or on various camp grounds. There's even one event held in the desert. Below are just a few of my favorites.

<u>Organizations</u>

<u>Institute of Pleasure</u>

I established the *Institute of Pleasure* in 2005 as an extension of the work I was already conducting in private practice with Sex Therapy, Relationship Coaching/Mentoring and education on sexual health. The *Institute of Pleasure* took my practice to the next level including Sex Research, Medical Physician and Mental Health practitioner education, as well as women's and couple's retreats. I also collaborated with other sexologists around the country and in Latin America. I developed *the Dominance and submission Therapy/Mentorship* model and began helping couples who wished to embrace this area of their lives. In 2010, we opened a new avenue for sex education by providing consultations and workshops specifically tailored to **writers** who needed assistance in technical/psychological aspects of BDSM to help them complete their novels. I look at this as a way to help further educate the public through *your books*—your accurate knowledge—as you share aspects of this unique and controversial lifestyle.

The *Institute of Pleasure* also provides education on sexual health to the general public; conducts therapeutic services in person, over the Internet or via phone; and conducts research on ancient cultures' sexual behavior/practices as well as those practices and behaviors of our generation. You will find various workshops offered dealing with BDSM as well as other relationship and self-empowerment workshops. Starting 2011 we will be conducting Webinars (virtual seminars held online) as many of our patients and participants live outside the New York City area. Visit www.bdsmforwriters.com or www.instituteofpleasure.org for more information.

<u>Carter Johnson Leather Library</u>

The Carter Johnson Leather Library is the only kinky library on wheels with over 10,000 pieces of Leather and Fetish memorabilia from the 1700's to the present. This unique library is a treasure trove of BDSM information, rare books on sexuality, articles, and even posters and commemorative pins. It began as the private collection of Viola Johnson who so elegantly stated in 2010 that she had gone from the "library's keeper and creator" to its "custodian", keeping the memory of the Leather Community's origins intact for generations to come.

Amazingly, Viola rescued many books from local landfills and from those that wanted to destroy the books, magazines and pamphlets due to their own prejudices and fears. The library's motto is: "Never again Landfill. Never again Flames." highlights the plight of the BDSM community as it struggles against the prejudices and social restrictions against it. As a non-profit 501(c)(3) organization, all donations to the Carter Johnson Leather Library are tax deductable. And of course, they accept anonymous donations.

Best of all, you can invite/hire this traveling library for your next author's event. Imagine the wealth of information you'll receive and provide to your participants. Plus, Mama Vi as Viola Johnson is known, will treat you with such loving care and respect as you sit with her and listen to how she found and rescued the books in her collection. I've no doubt you'll find incredible inspiration and create phenomenal characters. Visit www.leatherlibrary.org for more information.

BDSM for Writers Conference

BDSM for Writers Conference is a one-of-a-kind exclusive Three-Day intensive and interactive conference where writers are able to experience some of the fundamental basics of the BDSM community including playing with various toys and speaking with actual lifestyle practitioners. This combination of hands-on activities and panel discussion is designed to provide authors with a unique understanding of the BDSM lifestyle enabling them to write more credible BDMS romances, suspense, horror or any other genre. Each workshop is conducted in a closed area providing a safe empowering atmosphere in which to learn.

Plus, we look forward to teaming up with industry editors and agents who deal specifically with BDSM romances to provide you with an opportunity to pitch your story ideas and learn what they're looking to purchase.

An optional excursion to a local Fetish Club will be offer if there is one available in the area the Retreat is held in.

The *BDSM for Writers Conference* is an exclusive presentation by the *Institute of Pleasure* both for writers who are new to BDSM and are looking to write their first BDSM novel or for those with have years of experience. Each workshops is taught by experienced lifestyle practitioners, including some by world renowned Clinical Sexological, Dr. Charley Ferrer. To learn about the next upcoming *BDSM for Writers Conference* contact us at doctorcharley@bdsmforwriters.com or website my website www.bdsmforwriters.com.

Bondage Tours

Are you just curious or ready to explore? Visiting New York City and want a travel adventure to brag about or merely want a one-of-a-kind night to remember? If so join world renowned Clinical Sexologist, Dr. Charley Ferrer, for a one-of-a-kind night of sensual exploration into the lifestyle of Dominance and submission with her famous Bondage Tour. Our tour starts with an hour introduction on BDSM as well as the do's and don'ts allowed. Then it's off to a local BDSM nightclub to experience this unique lifestyle first hand. Dr. Charley will be available to answer any questions and concerns you might have. You are welcome to watch or participate during the evening as your heart desires. Dr. Charley strives to make this a fun, safe and discrete event. Couples as well as single men and women are encouraged to participate. No partner necessary! Everyone receives a copy of Dr. Charley's book, BDSM THE NAKED TRUTH, and a small gift to commemorate the night. This is a four hour event. Waivers will be signed because your safety is ultimately your concern. Must be over 19 years of age to participate! Visit www.bondagetours.com or write us at info@bondagetours.com for further information.

Master/slave Development Center

This program is run by Sir Stephen and Sir Eric. These two individuals to have a wealth of information related to the Master/slave union and BDSM Household development. Their courses are focused on the development of the **Master only** helping Him/Her address their personal and emotional growth as well as enhance interpersonal skills that enable the Master or

Mistress attain the levels of skills necessary for a more cohesive union between themselves and their slave. I attended their *One-Day Seminar for Masters* and found it the most useful workshop and discussion I've had in years, as it helped me further understand and solidify my decision and identification within this unique lifestyle.

The skills taught by the Master/slave Development Center provide a doorway into understanding yourself and your emotional desire to *JUST BE* putting you on the path to self-enlightenment as you establish your D/s relationship. To obtain further information about this valuable service, visit them at www.msdevelopmentcenter.com

National Coalition for Sexual Freedom (NCSF)

NCSF is a wonderful non-profit organization dedicated to the political, legal, and social rights and advocacy of consenting adults who engage in alternative sexual relationships and lifestyles. They provide direct services, education, advocacy, and outreach to directly benefit the BDSM, Leather, Fetish, Swing, and Polyamory communities. NCSF holds a wealth of legal information concerning the rights of an individual's sexual expression and can provide legal statues against consensual BDSM interactions in various states. A wonderful organization to support that is always in need of your financial donations. And as a 501(c) your donations are tax deductible. For further information visit them at www.ncsfreedom.com.

Catherine Gross, PCC

Catherine is an amazing woman who approaches life with such *joie de vive* that when I first met her, it made my heart smile. Her enthusiasm for helping others embrace their full potential in this lifestyle is inspiring. Through her popular workshops, *A Slave's Retreat* and *Foundations in Mastery*, Catherine helps men and women build the strong personal foundations that lead to creating healthy relationships. I recommend her as a resource to help you discover various aspects of the BDSM lifestyle and the personal struggles and ultimate self-acceptance of both the Master and slave. For further information visit her at www.bdsmclass.com or www.foryourlifecoach.com.

The Eulenspeigel Society (TES):

The Eulenspeigel Society is a non-profit 501(c)(3) organizations dedicated to the education and personal development of women and men in the Leather and BDSM communities. It is the oldest and largest BDSM support and education group in the US. TES offers a vast array of workshops and groups catering to Dominants and submissives, from both a male and female perspective. TES also has special interest groups geared toward subsets of the community such as Dominant women/submissive men; Dominant men/submissive women; TNG—the next generation (for individuals 35 years and under); Rope enthusiast; Switches; Spanking enthusiasts, and many more. TES also holds a yearly event for 4th July weekend at a local hotel in New Jersey that draws crowds from across the country. The amazing caliber of its presenters and the respectful community environment it has fostered is impressive. For further information visit www.tes.org .

ClubFEM International

ClubFEM International is an organization based on the premise of Dominant women/submissive men relationships. They provide education and activities for men and women throughout the US and abroad. I am most familiar with the New York City area Chapter and know there are chapters in almost every other city in the US—if not, you can always contact the organization and start one.

The beauty of ClubFEM is its dedication to providing a safe environment where Dominant women and submissive men can enjoy a little *Play* and socialize.

In 2010, ClubFEM in New York City hosted a Pony Romp in Central Park which we were able to film for my TV Talk show *PLEASURE*. Imagine "human ponies" ridden along the trails of this historical park creating an opportunity for the community to join in and/or ask questions. Such a marvelous experience, I'll never forget. There are many ClubFEM organizations throughout the US and overseas. Look on the

Internet and find the one nearest you. For further information visit www.clubfem.com/international.

<u>DomSub Friends</u>

Dom/sub Friends is an organization geared toward the BDSM community. It provides weekly demonstrations throughout the year on various topics of interest to the D/s and sex positive communities in the New York City area regardless of gender or sexual identity. As it holds its meetings at the oldest running Dungeon in the country, participants can have a night out that's not only educational but erotically fun as well. The one thing I love most about this organization is its organizer, Viktor, who is always quick with a joke and a smile and makes everyone feel welcomed. For further information visit www.domsubfriends.com.

<u>ShibariCon</u>

ShibariCon is the world's premier international pansexual event that caters to lovers of rope bondage. This event is held yearly in Chicago and provides amazing workshops. Its world class instructors are among the best in the US and abroad. The four day event provides hours of hands-on practice and even has *Play Space* so you can put those hours of training to good use. Though I have not personally had the opportunity to attend a ShibariCon event, I have spoken to a handful of participants who have; however it is several of the individual's I've seen demonstrating their rope skills who have presented at the event that leave me craving some free time to be able to attend. For further information visit www.shibaricon.comn.

Reading Material

The books I've mentioned below as well as those I've mentioned throughout the book are some of the best print resources on the market that I've personally read. By no means are they the only great ones available. I'm sure you'll find more on your own or if you have some you want to recommend, please feel free to email me or send me a copy. I'm always looking for more knowledge and information I can pass on to others.

Story of O by Pauline Reage

This is actually a very loving and romantic book featuring a Master/slave relationship. Though its focus is on the male dominant and submissive woman, the dynamics of the relationships are beautifully and erotically portrayed. There have been several movies made based on the book; however, I've found they all lack the emotional connection that the book chaptered. Then again, using your own imagination is so much more enticing.

Books by the Marquis de Sade

The Marquis de Sade wrote many books. One of the most popular was Justine. You might be interested to know that each addition of the book is somewhat different as are various other works by the Marquis. As the Marquis' books were re-written and his life took turns which damaged him emotionally, his stories took a harder twist and if you take into consideration his true love, his family circumstances, the period in which he lived (The French Revolution) and the corruption of church and government as well as the reign of Napoleon you may begin to see some of his writing in various lights. Though as one of the "fathers" of Sadomasochism, his legacy will live on in infamy.

The Latina Kama Sutra by Dr. Charley Ferrer

If you're writing a romance novel for the Spanish community this book is a must! *The Latina Kama Sutra* is the first sexuality book geared specifically toward the Latino community taking into consideration its unique culture, religion, and machismo; thus, providing subtle information about about Latinos that will help you experience the true flavor of your characters and target audience. Like the Hindu Kama Sutra from Vatsyayana, *The Latina Kama Sutra: The Ultimate Guide to Dating, Sex and Erotic Pleasure* is a dating manual which provides not only relationship and self-awareness exercises but provides an entire chapter on BDSM, its dynamics, its potential, and several erotic activities try with your partner.

Extreme Space: The Dominance and Submission Handbook by F.R.R. Mallory

Though this book is hard to find, it is a treasure trove of information into the phenomenon of *subspace* as well as *Domspace* and ways to work within it. The information in this book is valuable and realistic and addresses adverse reactions and *feral behavior* in submissives knowledge actually saved my butt once. Therefore, I recommend it to every Dominant I know. A definite must have!

The Forked Tongue by Flagg

If you want to know how to create those *Edge Play* and *Mind Fuck* scenarios we discussed, this book will leave you salivating and wondering why you didn't think of these possibilities sooner. The Forked Tongue will help you create scenes for your Dominant characters that will have your readers chaining you to your desk as they demand more of your wickedly erotic stories.

SM 101 by Jay Wiseman

This is the "entry" book into the community. It has wonderful information and safety tips as well as various ways to *play* and keep yourself in SSC mode. Though it can get a little preachy on safety issues, it's a good read. This book was my intellectual or should I say academic introduction into the BDMS community when I first discovered it in San Francisco while working on my Doctorate in Human Sexuality.

Different Loving: The World of Sexual Dominance and Submission by Gloria Brame

This is a huge book on the various aspects of BDSM. What I love most about this book is that it provides you with insight into the mind of the Dominant and the submissive by allowing you to read their words and thoughts. This book will provide you with amazing insight into the emotional connections individuals make in this unique community as you read "their word" and how various activities affected them.

The Sexually Dominant Woman: A Handbook for the Nervous Beginner by Lady Green

This book provides you with wonderful ideas to help your Dominant character get started. Don't worry that it's written for women, men can learn from it as well.

The Mistress Manual: The Good Girl's Guide to Female Dominance by Mistress Lorelei

Another wonderful book on how to embrace your Dominant side whether as a man or woman. Definitely worth reading twice and taking notes.

Family Jewels: A Guide to Male Genital Play and Torment by Hardy Haberman

A must read if you want to explore controlling a man in the psychological realms through his most prized possession—his cock! Hardy provides you with fantastic ideas on how to torment your lover (your character) in his "family jewels" and how to control his every move. This book is surprisingly in-depth and covers techniques as well as the psychological aspects related to the male psyche.

Videos

Videos are always a wonderful resource for you especially if your time is limited and you don't have hours available to read. There are wonderful videos available for things like bondage or mummification and a whole host of other D/s activities. BDMS videos featuring actual D/s scenes are an individual preference. Unfortunately, many of the ones on the market are just tacky, unrealistic, or specifically created for titillation. To find a good Dominant woman/submissive man's video you'll have to hunt for it. However, don't feel guilty about indulging your voyeuristic needs—enjoy!

There are two videos I've noted below which are the best BDSM themed videos on the mainstream market that depict

Dominance and submission from a somewhat positive perspective though they still have their short comings, these are Secretary and Killing Me Softly.

Secretary starring James Spader & Maggie Gyllenhaal,
    This amazing movie is not only touchingly romantic; it's tastefully erotic as well. It provides you with a wonderful look at the struggles these two individuals experienced in their attempt to discover who they are and become comfortable with their sexual desires. I especially enjoy watching the heartfelt performance by James Spader as he struggles with his need to dominate his secretary and yet conform to society's norms. Often this internal struggle a Master/Mistress undergoes to accept their dominant nature despite the dictates of societal norms (especially for a woman) is not accurately portrayed and is one of the most important facets in the make-up of the individual and leads to the foundation of the relationships they'll share with another. This movie portrays this internal struggle brilliantly.

Killing Me Softly starring Heather Graham & Joseph Fiennes
    This erotic portrayal of a couple embracing their BDSM connection held a few of the dynamics which you'll encounter when entering into such a relationship. The passion. The obsession. The need to connect with all aspects of the other individual's life. An amazing performance by Joseph Fiennes. And the *Breath Play Scene* they engage in will make you hit the rewind button several times.
    However, the down side to this film is that she starts questioning whether she's "sick" for wanting to submit to him which is unfortunately a common theme in books and movies trying to portray the BDSM lifestyle.

Romance Novels

I tend to be very selective and loyal in my romance readings especially when I read a book for its BDSM storyline. I want to read a credible D/s story not something which makes me argue with the storyline as I know the Dominant and/or submissive wouldn't really behave in such a manner in real life.

My time is valuable, I want **believable** fantasy. That said, if you want to see great BDSM stories in action not to mention phenomenal storytelling, I'd recommend my all time favorite author, Joey W. Hill, who has a marvelous way of showing and combining the psychological make-up and desires of both the Dominant and the submissive. Her Vampire series is a phenomenal and erotically tasty treat with open and honest depictions of various BDSM interactions.

Lora Leigh's Breed series, in my opinion, actually holds a lot of dominance and submission qualities and undertones and is another of my favorite books to read for its strong sexual content and believable characters.

Jessica Lust, though not well known is an amazing BDSM writer. She tends to write on "forbidden" topics such as *adult age play* and more hard core sadomasochistic interactions which is why she isn't in the main stream circles. However, you can find a few of her short stories through the *Institute of Pleasure* and loyal friends.

The most amazing thing about Jessica's writing is her unique approach. Unlike other writers, Jessica interviews her "readers" then creates a short story just for them. Thus every book she writes is specifically tailored to the primary reader's desires. Jessica writes the book from the point of view of the reader or the opposite character making you feel as if you're peaking into the individual's private diary. It's an amazing concept in writing! As each story is commissioned by a specific reader, the books are rare indeed.

I'm sure you have your own favorites or will soon. Perhaps you might become another one of mine! I'm always looking for a great BDSM romance though my preference is the alpha male submissive and his Dominant Lady. Hint! Hint!

In conclusion:

BDSM is like the ocean. It is forever moving, changing, evolving within you and when you're not respectful of it, it'll drag you across its bottom and try to drown you. That said it can be such fun playing in its waters, diving into its waves and exploring all the potential possibilities that you are as a person— that your characters are. You'll never find the same freedom in any other relationship that you discovered in this one.

It is my sincere hope that as with any other genre you have decided to write within, you will do your homework—your research—to ensure you present your readers with accurate information on this lifestyle.

As we all know, it's common to believe what we read and nowhere is this more dangerous to an individual than with BDSM novels because in this case the reader may not only believe the information you provide—whether in desire or prejudice—but he/she may also attempt to mimic the *Scenes* you describe.

I recently sat in on a panel discussion with accomplished authors who wrote *Dominance and submission* novels and though the majority of the writers did not actively participate in BDSM practices, several had diligently conducted their research. One popular writer surprised me greatly when she adamantly stated that she was "writing fantasy" and her readers "should know that", thus it didn't matter whether she understood the lifestyle or its dynamics. And though she does have a point, you are writing fiction—erotic fantasy—as writers, you also have an obligation to your readers to at the very least respect the topics you write about especially if it's a way of life. I seriously doubt any author today would write a book with blatant disrespect for someone's ethnicity or sexual orientation—the same respect and accuracy should be afforded to the BDSM community.

Keep in mind that to thousands of men and women, *Dominance and submission* is not merely a kink but a way of life. It is how he and she identify themselves and how they live their lives and interact with their lovers, friends and life partners/spouses. BDSM is sacred to them!

Never forget that, for some readers, your book may be their introduction to BDSM and thus you become the expert and the judge of whether they are "normal" or not.

Allow yourself to explore as you conduct your research; after all, you have the perfect excuse now—*You're doing Research*! Join organizations, interview individuals in the lifestyle, go to workshops, even contact me at the *Institute of Pleasure* and join one of our upcoming *BDSM for Writers Conference* and/or any of the other wonderful resources available out there.

I hope that *BDSM for Writers* was able to provide you with a comprehensive insight into this unique lifestyle. I welcome your comments on this or any other one of my books. May your writing flow freely and bountiful!

Live with passion,

Doctor Charley...

Special Thanks to our supporters for donating prizes and
services
Captured Erotica www.capturederotica.com
Dungeon Delights www.dungeondelights.com
Quality Whips www.qualitywhips.com
Skylar Kade www.skylarkade.com

About the author

Dr. Charley Ferrer is a world-renowned Clinical Sexologist, Radio/TV Producer, and award winning author. She is highly sought after for her expertise on relationships, sexuality, and sensual self-acceptance throughout the US and Latin America. Her television show PLEASURE has been nominated for Best TV Talk Show 2007 and Best Northeast Regional show in 2008. Dr. Charley has a private practice in New York City and provides coaching and consultations on various aspects of sexuality including Sex Therapy, BDSM, and self-empowerment both in person and over the phone/Internet.

Dr. Charley is the Sex Expert for various radio and televisions programs in both English and Spanish including Fox News Latino, Univision, Kiss FM the Michael Baisden Show, and many others.

Visit her website www.bdsmforwriters or www.instituteofpleasure.org more information.

29556944R00116

Made in the USA
Lexington, KY
29 January 2014